LOUISVILLE LANDMARKS

A Viewbook of Architectural and Historic Landmarks in Louisville, Kentucky

JOANNE WEETER
Historic Preservation Officer
Louisville-Jefferson County Metro

BUTLER BOOKS
LOUISVILLE

This viewbook showcasing Louisville Metro's strong commitment to preserving and protecting the area's historic, architectural and cultural resources is dedicated to the members, both present and past, of the Historic Landmarks and Preservation Districts Commission for their years of stewardship and diligence.

Special thanks go to my colleagues and fellow staff members for their insightful comments and guidance on the book's accuracy and contents.

Joanne Weeter
Historic Preservation Officer
Planning and Design Services

Louisville-Jefferson County Metro
Jerry E. Abramson, Mayor
Louisville Metro Council

Cover photo credits:Union Station courtesy of Louisville Metro Planning and Design; City Hall, Wolf Pen Branch Mill. and Cherokee Triangle courtesy of University of Louisville Photographic Archives

ISBN 1-884532-62-4

Published by Butler Books
P.O. Box 7311
Louisville, KY 40207
www.butlerbooks.com

Printed in Canada by Friesens Printers
through Four Colour Imports, Louisville, KY

LOUISVILLE LANDMARKS
Contents

An Overview of the City of Louisville's Historical Development

The City of Louisville, the largest city in the Commonwealth of Kentucky, was founded in 1778 by explorer George Rogers Clark and later named in honor of French King Louis XVI. The City owes its existence to the Falls of the Ohio, a two mile long series of rapids and the only natural impediment to navigation of the entire length of the Ohio River. The river was an early transportation route for travel to and from the east. Because of the falls, cargo had to be portaged by land. Naturally, warehousing, wholesaling of goods, hotels and hostelries sprang up in response. Thus, Louisville became a stopover point, a vital conduit for travel, and a hub of commercial activity. The steamboat contributed to the Falls City's growth and prosperity, and by 1850 made Louisville the tenth largest city in the nation.

In the mid-1800s the railroad supplanted the steamboat as the preferred mode of transportation. Louisville's extensive system of rail lines to areas north and south made Kentucky, a border state with allegiances to the North, a major supplier of goods during the Civil War. It also secured her place as the prosperous "Gateway to the South" during the post-war period.

Soon an industrial economic base replaced the mercantile trade of Louisville's earliest years. Tobacco processing and distilling were overshadowed by industrial manufacturing of agricultural implements, iron pipe, furniture and cement. The compact mixed-use city of the early-to-mid-1800s blossomed during the last thirty years of the nineteenth century as electric streetcar lines made areas outside the city core more easily accessible. City boundaries and infrastructure expanded proportionately as residential, commercial, and industrial uses became more geographically segregated. Automobile usage in the 1920s and beyond led to further expansion of Louisville's municipal boundaries.

An industrial decline during this period was reversed by World War II, as almost all of the city's industrial resources were converted to military production. Later, post-war defense plants were converted to peacetime production, and Louisville became the leading industrial center of the southeast.

In the 1950s the automobile continued to affect Louisville as services moved away from the city core to outlying suburbs. By the 1960s construction in Louisville's central business district had come to a virtual halt, and many stores, hotels, and entertainment-related venues were closed. Manufacturing also declined sharply, but has been replaced in more recent years by office-related uses, especially in the city's core.

Despite the decline in urban population and the deterioration and/or demolition of select urban neighborhoods, the Louisville metro area overall has remained remarkably intact. In fact, the city has been widely recognized by visitors and residents alike in recent years for its wealth of historic resources. From the cast-iron storefronts along Main Street and the old tobacco warehouses on Market, to the cozy craftsman bungalows and working class shotgun houses, the city offers tremendous architectural quality and variety. Recognition of the importance of Louisville's historic past, through tangible evidence provided by buildings, structures and sites, offers a unique opportunity to learn from the past. It is these resources that the historic preservation movement has sought to protect.

American Life and Accident Insurance Company

Photo by Louisville Metro Planning and Design

Location/Address: Fifth and Main Streets (north side)
Date: 1973
Style: International Style
Architect/Builder: Ludwig Mies van der Rohe

The American Life and Accident Insurance Company building was built adjacent to the Belvedere at Fifth and Main Streets in 1969 for local businessman Dinwiddie Lampton, Jr., to serve as the headquarters for his Kentucky-based insurance company. Internationally-recognized German émigré and architect Ludwig Mies van der Rohe (1886-1969) designed the building. This sleek, simple cube-like structure of glass and Cor-ten steel, a material intended to weather to a rust-like finish, is the epitome of the Mies philosophy that "less is more." Here, the structure of the building is visibly expressed and celebrated by the use of vertical and horizontal steel bands punctuated by large, bronze-tinted plate glass windows. It was completed four years after the architect's death. It is the only building in Kentucky designed by Mies, widely acknowledged as a leader of the modern architecture movement.

This view of the building is from its north side, which faces Louisville's Belvedere and the Ohio River. Opposite: The "front" (south) side of the building from Main Street.

BANK OF LOUISVILLE BUILDING/ ACTORS THEATRE OF LOUISVILLE

Location/Address:	316-28 West Main Street
Date:	Circa 1837
Style:	Greek Revival
Architects/Builders:	James H. Dakin, with renovation and new construction by Harry Weese and Associates
Historic Status:	National Historic Landmark, Metro Landmark District, National Register of Historic Places

Prominent 19th century architect James H. Dakin designed this former bank building in the Greek Revival style, popular during the mid-1800s because of its association with democratic ideals. This building is considered one of the finest small-scale examples of Greek Revival style architecture in America. The architect successfully conveys formality through both symmetry and simplicity of design and materials. This two-story, stone-faced building is dominated by a pair of fluted, colossal Ionic columns set between battered walls that are topped by a plain entablature. Extra architectural punch is added to the building's otherwise plain façade through the use of architectural ornamentation, most notably anthemion, inspired by the popular 19th century pattern books of Minard Lafever. The interior features a domed, coffered banking room. Ironically, this structure is best viewed from the second-floor lobby of the relatively new Galt House East building located directly across the street. Since 1972 this former bank building has housed the world-renowned Actors Theatre of Louisville (ATL), one of the nation's most respected regional theater companies. Designated the State Theatre of Kentucky in 1974, ATL is known for both the quality and innovation of its productions.

The building is now known throughout the theatrical world as the home of Actors Theatre of Louisville and the Humana Festival of New American Plays.

BELLE OF LOUISVILLE

Location/Address:	Fourth Street at River Road
Date:	1914
Style:	Sternwheeler Day Packet and Excursion Boat
Architect/Builder:	James Rees & Sons
Historic Status:	National Historic Landmark, Metro Landmark, National Register of Historic Places

The *Belle of Louisville* is a steam-powered, sternwheel-propelled excursion boat. The *Belle* was originally named the *Idlewild* and was built in 1914 by James Rees and Sons of Pittsburgh. She began as a ferry and day packet and was outfitted as an occasional excursion boat as well. In 1962, Jefferson County Judge Marlow Cook and Louisville Mayor Charles Farnsley purchased the vessel (renamed the *Avalon* in 1948) to help Louisville and Jefferson County reclaim its cultural and historical links with the Ohio River. She was formally christened the *Belle of Louisville* in that same year. The *Belle* is listed in the National Register of Historic Places and is a National Historic Landmark based on her significance to the history of maritime navigation on the Western Rivers and as the sole remaining Western Rivers day packet. She is the oldest operating river steamboat in the world.

In this pre-1948 photograph, the ship now known as The Belle of Louisville *was called the* Idlewild, *and here is seen taking on passengers for a river excursion.*

The Mayor Andrew Broaddus *is the only surviving inland lifesaving station in the United States. It is now the wharf boat and business office for the* Belle of Louisville.

MAYOR ANDREW BROADDUS WHARF BOAT/
COAST GUARD STATION #10

Location/Address:	Fourth Street at River Road
Date:	1928
Style:	Steel-hulled Houseboat Life Saving Station
Architect/Builder:	Shipyard, Dubuque, Iowa
Historic Status:	National Historic Landmark, National Register of Historic Places

The *Mayor Andrew Broaddus* was named in honor of Louisville's mayor (1900-1972) who served from 1953 to 1958. She is a direct descendant of an earlier 1881 lifesaving station and the only extant floating lifesaving station built to aid shipwrecked mariners and endangered cargo near the Falls of the Ohio. Before becoming the wharf boat and business office for the *Belle of Louisville*, this vessel served as *Life Saving Station #10*. When the lifesavers were called to save those who were in peril at the Falls of the Ohio, their skiffs were launched from this vessel. John F. Gillooly (often called either "Captain Jack" or "Hero of the Falls"), the most famous lifesaver to serve on the *Broaddus*, was reportedly responsible for saving 6,312 lives, $5 million dollars worth of cargo, and recovering the bodies of 40 drowning victims during a career that spanned from about 1870 to his retirement in 1917. It was Gillooly and two others, Captain Billy Devan and John Tully, whose rescue in 1880 of 75 people from the steamer *Virgie Lee* prompted the United States government to establish *Life Saving Station # 10* as the nation's first inland lifesaving station. All three were awarded gold medals of honor by a special act of Congress for their heroics. In 1915 the Life Saving Service and the Revenue Cutter Service were combined into the U.S. Coast Guard. The *Broaddus* was declared a National Historic Landmark for its association with maritime history and is the only surviving inland lifesaving station in the United States.

BELLEVIEW

Location/Address:	6600 River Road
Dates:	Circa 1855, 1865
Style:	Transitional Greek Revival
Architects/Builders:	Joseph Bell, owner (circa 1855);
	Henry Bell, owner-heir (1865)
Historic Status:	National Register of Historic Places

Belleview rests on a large parcel of land located on the Ohio River and was built by farmer Joseph Bell around 1855. Bell, also a grocer and commission merchant, constructed the brick, two-story, single-pile I house after purchase of land for his farm from the Transylvania Seminary in 1854. Two years after the house's construction Bell died, leaving the farm to his wife and two sons. It was his son, Henry, in counsel with his mother, Selena A. Bell, who assumed authority over the farm and, around 1865, developed it into a gentleman farm. Henry constructed the two-story, double-pile brick addition to that built by his father, thereby creating a unified assembly. He also is responsible for reorientation of the dwelling with principal facades facing both the Ohio River and River Road. Such an orientation signifies the importance of travel by river and road. The farm complex has a number of major and minor structures and outbuildings (the domestic complex includes the main dwelling, smoke house, and a carriage house/garage while the agricultural complex includes a barn, corn crib, and tenant house). However it is the farmhouse itself that is truly outstanding. Its significance lies in the fact that it displays stylistic traits that are atypical of Kentucky. The house was designed to reflect regional stylistic tendencies of houses found in upstate New York, home to Henry Bell's parents. While others in the Jefferson County area were building houses in the favored Greek Revival or Italianate styles, Bell selected a house type associated with northern sensibilities. Multi-paned casement windows on the river façade, for instance, are a more common stylistic trait of houses in northern locales.

These views show Belleview's west (river-facing) entrance (above), and the east entrance facing River Road (below).

The Brennan House is a rare vestige of Louisville's Victorian era, and survives intact on Fifth Street as a residential island surrounded by downtown Louisville.

BRENNAN HOUSE

Location/Address:	631 South Fifth Street
Date:	1868
Style:	Italianate
Architect/Builder:	Unknown, although it is reminiscent of works by Louisville architect Henry Whitestone
Historic Status:	Metro Landmark, National Register of Historic Places

The Brennan House is a three-story brick townhouse constructed in the Italianate style. Although constructed by tobacco merchant Francis S. J. Ronald, it takes its name from the Thomas Brennan family, longest occupants at this address. It represents townhouse living in Victorian Louisville and is one of the last surviving Victorian residences still standing in the metro area's downtown. Surprisingly, it has survived in a period of widespread urban expansion in Louisville's downtown and has an interior that remains virtually intact. Even more remarkable, however, is the fact that the house is furnished with the personal effects of the Brennans who lived here from 1884 to 1969. Worldly and well-traveled, the Brennan collection includes gilt-framed mirrors, Tiffany lamps, and a ten-foot-tall walnut hat rack. After the last Brennan died, the house and its furnishings were bequeathed to the Filson Club (now Filson Historical Society). The Filson managed the house until 1992 when it was sold to Brennan House, Inc., a private foundation.

THE BROWN HOTEL

Location/Address:	335 West Broadway (Fourth and Broadway)
Date:	1923
Style:	Colonial Revival
Architect/Builder:	Preston J. Bradshaw
Historic Status:	National Register of Historic Places

James Graham Brown built the Brown Hotel in 1923 at the "magic corner" of Fourth Street and Broadway. Its construction marked the rise of Broadway as the commercial focal point of downtown Louisville and soon after construction attracted commercial office buildings to the area (the Heyburn Building, the Fincastle Building, and the Martin Brown/Commonwealth Building, now demolished). Adjacent to the hotel on Broadway, Brown also built the Brown Building in 1925 and the Brown Theater in 1926. Well-known hotel architect Preston J. Bradshaw, designer of three hotels in St. Louis (the Chase Hotel, Coronado Hotel, and Embassy Hotel), conceived the design. It was built of matte-faced brown brick with limestone and terra cotta trim in the Colonial Revival style. Twelve hundred workers finished it in a record twelve months time. After lavish opening ceremonies presided over by Judge Robert W. Bingham, former Prime Minister of England David Lloyd George became the first person to sign the guest register. Architect Bradshaw remarked at the opening ceremonies that, "This is the first instance on record in which an owner and the architect are on speaking terms at the finish." This 600-room facility was designed with restaurants and shops on the ground level with banquet rooms, ballrooms and hotel rooms above. Parts of the first and second floors housed the lobby, barbershop, billiard room, Turkish bath, lounges, offices, restaurant and the ballroom. The lobby is English Renaissance Revival in style; the Grill Room is Elizabethan; and the dining room is Adamesque.

The Brown Hotel, on the corner of Fourth and Broadway, has anchored the southern end of the bustling Fourth Street commercial corridor for more than 80 years.

THEODORE BROWN HOUSE/WOODHAVEN

Photo by Eric Butler

Location/Address:	401 South Hubbards Lane
Date:	1853
Style:	Gothic Revival
Architect/Builder:	Theodore Brown
Historic Status:	National Register of Historic Places

The Theodore Brown House was constructed in eastern Jefferson County in 1853. It is a symmetrical, five-bay, two-story structure built of brick arranged in a Flemish bond pattern. It has a central projecting entry bay adorned with a recessed entry on the ground level, a bay window above, and is topped by a front-facing gable. Two recessed bays flank this arrangement. The building's appearance is unified by both a Gothic Revival style one-story porch and by decorative bargeboard trimming the front facing gable end. Similar Gothic inspired detailing is found on the building's sides and rear. This building is a striking example of the influence of Romantic Victorian-era architect A.J. Downing, who achieved fame through the authorship and publication of numerous architectural pattern books that influenced a countless number of builders and homeowners during the late 19th century. Twentieth century modifications to the house and grounds include a porch addition and a substantial two-story rear wing. Outbuildings include a two-story brick carriage house and a newly-constructed octagonal brick outbuilding that services the building's present use as a bed-and-breakfast inn. The building's namesake, Theodore Brown, was the son of James Brown who came to Jefferson County from Delaware. The house was built after Theodore inherited part of his father's estate.

Theodore Brown House, circa 1930s. Opposite: Known today as Woodhaven, the house is a well-known bed-and-breakfast inn.

By 1841, Butchertown's street system was laid out and the area's future was secure. Most of the workers in the butcher-related industries lived in the Butchertown neighborhood area as well. Thus, it developed a mixed-use character early in its history with residences standing side-by-side with commercial concerns.

██ BUTCHERTOWN DISTRICT ██

Location/Address:	East of Louisville's Central Business District and bordered by the Ohio River, Interstate 65, Main Street, Mellwood Avenue, and Beargrass Creek.
Dates:	Early 1800s up to the early 1900s
Style:	Eclectic
Architect/Builder:	Multiple
Historic Status:	Metro Landmark District, National Register of Historic Places

Butchertown's early origins can be traced to Henry Fait, who established one of the area's first gristmills in the area. He was soon followed by Colonel Frederick Geiger, who established a flour mill, operated a ferry between southern Indiana and Louisville, and built a 20-room farmhouse around 1800.

Because of the water provided by Beargrass Creek and the presence of a turnpike, butchering soon developed in the area. By 1834 the Bourbon Stockyards, a major local slaughterhouse, was built, securing the Butchertown neighborhood's role as the home to the city's principal butchering and slaughtering industries. Cattle drovers from as far away as central Kentucky herded their animals along the nearby turnpike roads to the stockyards.

Toward the end of the 1900s large meatpacking plants moved into the area and skewed the land usage toward industrial as they replaced small butchering concerns. The incompatibility between the increase in industrial developments alongside existing residential uses resulted in homeowner disinvestments. The 1937 flood that damaged or destroyed many buildings in the area hastened the area's decline. In later years, a floodwall was constructed that further severed ties between the neighborhood and the river to the north.

In the 1960s, neighborhood residents formed Butchertown, Inc., a neighborhood revitalization organization. They convinced the city's planning authorities to revert some industrially-zoned land to residential zoning to more accurately reflect original functions and current use. The efforts paid off slowly but surely. In 1976, the area was listed in the National Register of Historic Places and in 2003, Butchertown was designated a Metro Landmark District.

Main Branch of the Louisville Free Public Library, 301 York Street, shown circa 1908. The flagship of the nine-branch library system, the Main Branch is an outstanding example of Beaux-Arts Classicism. Pilcher and Tachau, a New York firm selected after an invitational competition, built it. It still serves as the main branch of the library system.

CARNEGIE LIBRARIES/MAIN BRANCH

- Crescent Hill Branch (1908), 2762 Frankfort Avenue, Thomas and Bohne, architects
- Eastern Branch (1914), Corner of Hancock and Lampton Streets, Fred Erhart, architect
- Highland Branch (1908), 1000 Cherokee Road, Hutchings and Hawes, architects
- Jefferson Branch (1913), 1718 West Jefferson Street, D.X. Murphy, architect
- Main Branch (1908), 301 York Street, Pilcher and Tachau, architects
- Parkland Branch (1908), 2743 Virginia Avenue, Brinton B. Davis, architect
- Portland Branch (1913), 3305 Northwestern Parkway, Valentine Peers Collins, architect
- Shelby Park Branch (1911), 600 East Oak Street, Loomis and Hartman, architects
- Western Branch (1908), 604 South Tenth Street, McDonald and Dodd, architects

Historic Status: All local Carnegie Libraries are Metro Landmarks except the Jefferson Branch. All are listed in the National Register of Historic Places.

Between 1886 and 1921, over 1,789 libraries across the nation were constructed with financial assistance from industrialist and philanthropist Andrew Carnegie (1835-1919). Typically, under the Carnegie philanthropic approach, local municipalities signed a written agreement to provide the land for the library building and also assured that, once built, the library would receive long-term maintenance. Carnegie in turn provided the money for the "bricks and mortar." Louisville took advantage of the philanthropist's planned giving with great gusto. The citizens wrote to Carnegie, agreed to his terms, and eventually built nine public libraries between 1908 and 1914 with Carnegie funds. Louisville's Carnegie Libraries are classically inspired architectural gems designed by a veritable "Who's Who" list of Kentucky architects. They are tangible reminders of one of America's greatest social movements–the establishment of a library system "free to all."

Contrary to popular belief, Andrew Carnegie himself did not dictate building design. Instead, he left design decisions up to the local communities. Many selected to erect Classical Revival style buildings that they felt embodied ideals of democracy, an image they wanted to project to the community at large. All local Carnegie-endowed libraries in Louisville fit a similar profile; all were built in or close to the city's urban core area to serve residents of turn-of-the-century streetcar suburbs; all were built of masonry both for durability and to project an air of importance; all have rectangular, cube-like massing; all are one- or two-stories in height; all rest upon a raised basement level to create an air of prominence; all are formal and symmetrical in design; and all are architect-designed.

CATHEDRAL OF THE ASSUMPTION

Location/Address:	433-43 South Fifth Street
Dates:	1849-52
Style:	Gothic Revival, church (1849); Italianate parish school (1867); Italianate with Tudor elements, rectory (1912)
Architects/Builders:	William Keely (church); Henry Whitestone and Isaiah Rogers (tower), D.X. Murphy (renovation), Lawrence Melillo (renovation)
Historic Status:	Metro Landmark, National Register of Historic Places

The Cathedral of the Assumption, seat of the Roman Catholic Archdiocese of Louisville, has been the focal point for Louisville's Roman Catholic community since 1852, the year of its dedication. It is the oldest inland diocese in the nation. Church architect William Keely, whose work can be seen throughout the Commonwealth of Kentucky, designed the structure. He is considered one of the nation's leading Catholic architects of the mid-nineteenth century. The focal point of Keely's Gothic Revival-style design is the symmetry of its façade that features a slender central spire adorned with ornate stone detailing. Interior treatments include decorative plasterwork by Patrick Bannon. Highlights in the Cathedral's long and notable history include the unsuccessful search for armed men during the Bloody Monday Riot of 1855; the 1862 service to honor both Confederate and Union casualties of the Civil War; and the aid provided to refugees of the devastating 1937 flood.

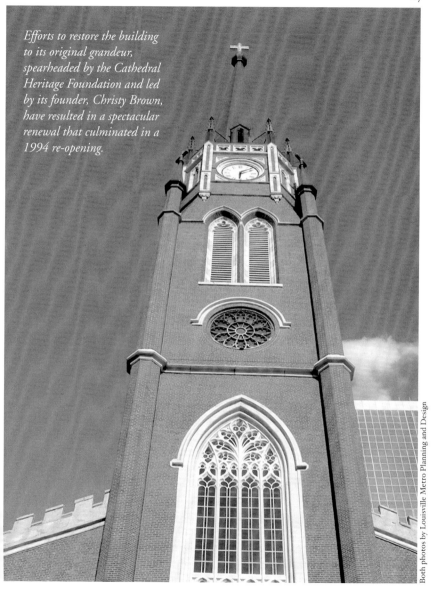

Efforts to restore the building to its original grandeur, spearheaded by the Cathedral Heritage Foundation and led by its founder, Christy Brown, have resulted in a spectacular renewal that culminated in a 1994 re-opening.

Both photos by Louisville Metro Planning and Design

CAVE HILL CEMETERY

Location/Address:	Northeast of the intersection of Broadway, Baxter Avenue and Bardstown Road
Date:	Established 1835
Style:	Victorian Romanticism
Architects/Builders:	Cemetery engineers/landscape architects include David Ross (1848–1856); Robert Ross (1856–1890); Robert Campbell (1890–1938); Ira Mitchell (1938–1974); Leroy Squires (1974–present)
Historic Status:	National Register of Historic Places

Cave Hill Cemetery, which now comprises over 300 acres, was established by the City of Louisville in 1835. The name Cave Hill is derived from the name given the farm by the site's original owner prior to the city's purchase for use as a cemetery. Soon after city acquisition, the Cave Hill Investment Company was formalized to ensure the perpetual care of the cemetery and its lots. Cave Hill was designed in keeping with the traditions of 19th century English landscape gardening designs. Superintendent Leroy F. Squires equates the cemetery with "…a controlled, naturalistic landscape with many natural features as landscape accents, as well as more refined and formal areas to create landscape interest and plant diversity on the grounds." Scottish landscape gardener David Ross first laid out the cemetery. Ross evaluated the natural contour of the land and developed a geomorphic concept that took advantage of the area's naturally existing trees, hills, valleys, lakes and sinkholes. The Ross design approach was carried forth after his death by his successors. Under the direction of Robert Campbell, a man-made lake, superintendent's office, reading room and rustic shelter house were added in 1890.

The gravestones provide a veritable "Who's Who" of Louisville. Markers erected prior to 1900 reflect an age when there was great competition to erect the most magnificent marker to honor a loved one. The area's leading architects designed a number of them. The Temple of Love, erected by the Satterwhite family, is one of Cave Hill's most magnificent. Mausoleums are prevalent as well and many are ornately stone-carved confections. A national cemetery is located within the boundary of Cave Hill with pointed markers denoting Confederate dead and rounded markers indicating Union dead.

Pictured is the main entrance into Cave Hill Cemetery. The magnificent monumental statuary serves not only as a monument to the deceased but to the skill and craftsmanship of the architects, sculptors and artists who conceived them.

CHEROKEE TRIANGLE DISTRICT

Location/Address:	Roughly bounded by Grinstead Drive, Cherokee Park, Eastern Parkway, and Bardstown Road
Dates:	1880s-1920s
Style:	Late Victorian Eclectic styles (Italianate, Queen Anne, Greek Revival, Tudor, and Craftsman style structures predominate)
Architect/Builder:	Multiple
Historic Status:	Metro Landmark District, National Register of Historic Places

Surveyors James Henning and Joshua Speed established the Cherokee Triangle neighborhood, east of Louisville's downtown, in 1871. It takes its name from the triangular shape of the neighborhood. The area developed as a residential enclave intended as an escape from the noise and soot of the city. It developed slowly at first because transportation to and from the area was limited to horse and buggy, a luxury only the elite could afford. Arrival of electric trolleys in 1889, however, allowed for easy access from the Triangle to the city's business district.

Cherokee Park's opening in 1892 added immensely to the Cherokee Triangle neighborhood's appeal. Designed by nationally-recognized landscape architect Frederick Law Olmsted, it was a welcome amenity to the area's growing managerial class. In fact, a statue of John B. Castleman, President of the Board of Parks Commission, who helped create the city's park system, stands at the intersection of Cherokee Road and Cherokee Parkway.

Nearby Bardstown Road, a former turnpike, allowed for commercial development outside the confines of the residential Cherokee Triangle. By the late 1940s the area had lost some appeal as outlying suburbs came into favor. By the 1950s and into the 1960s the area was feeling a steady decline with many of the area's larger homes either subdivided into apartments or demolished for multi-family new construction. By the 1970s, however, the Cherokee Triangle Association was formed, the neighborhood was listed in the National Register of Historic Places, and the area was designated a Metro Landmark District. It has once again become one of Louisville's most sought-after addresses.

Many Cherokee Triangle residents and institutions selected the leading local architects of the day to design their late Victorian confections in a variety of eclectic revival styles. Apartment complexes and institutions dot the streetscape. Italianate, Queen Anne, Greek Revival, Tudor, and Craftsman-style structures predominate.

The Cathedral complex underwent a major restoration and renovation between 1997 and 2002.

CHRIST CHURCH CATHEDRAL

Location/Address:	421 South Second Street
Dates:	1824-1912
Style:	Gothic Revival
Architects/Builders:	Church by Graham and Ferguson (1824), with alterations/additions by John Stirewalt (1845), William H. Redin (1859, 1870); Cathedral House by John Bacon Hutchings and Sons (1912); Cloister Garden (1957); John Milner and Associates, Inc, renovation/restoration (1997-2005)
Historic Status:	Metro Landmark, National Register of Historic Places

Christ Church Cathedral, Louisville's oldest church building in continuous use, became the Cathedral of the Kentucky Episcopal Diocese in 1894. The complex is comprised of a cathedral, cloister garden, and cathedral house. The recent acquisition of an 1830 residence next to the Cathedral complex completes the grouping. The first structure built in the complex was an 1824 Federal-style meeting house of brick construction with a timber truss roof designed by Graham and Ferguson. An addition to the 1824 structure, designed by architect John Stirewalt, was completed in 1846. During this building campaign, the church's east end was enlarged. In 1859, a chancel was constructed. A major architectural feature of the reconfiguration of the building's main entrance occurred in 1870. This involved the demolition of the original west facade and bell tower and construction of the present limestone facade with two towers. Redesigned in the Gothic Revival style, the centered entryway is topped by an arched second-floor tripartite window arrangement with a cross at its peak. Flanking this arrangement are towers of differing heights: an ornate spire surmounts the north tower while the higher south tower is topped by a squared roofline arrangement. Noted English-born architect William H. Redin, who by the late 1850s was a favored local architect, designed both. Installation of stained glass memorial windows, some designed by the Tiffany Glass and Decorating Company of New York, were installed in the 1880s through the end of the 19th century. By 1912, a Cathedral House was constructed south of the church proper based on plans drawn by John Bacon Hutchings and Sons, a local architectural firm.

CHURCHILL DOWNS

Location/Address:	700 Central Avenue
Dates:	1874 with additions in the 1920s, 1960s, and again in 2003 and 2004
Style:	Neo-Georgian
Architects/Builders:	D.X. Murphy and Company, with alterations and additions by Luckett & Farley
Historic Status:	National Historic Landmark, National Register of Historic Places

Horses have played an important role in Kentucky's economy as a means of transport and later as an agribusiness and a sport. Meriwether Lewis Clark, Jr., the grandson of William Clark of the famed Lewis and Clark Expedition, established Churchill Downs in 1875 in an effort to showcase high quality thoroughbreds from Kentucky breeding farms. The track was initially known as the Louisville Jockey Club and showcased races that were modeled after racing classics that Clark had witnessed at Britain's famed Epsom Downs during a tour of Europe. Those races included the Kentucky Derby, a race for three-year-old thoroughbreds inspired by the Epsom Derby, the English classic for horses of that age group. After a strong start, the Kentucky Derby and the track struggled in the late 1800s, but both recovered and the Kentucky Derby has become America's most prominent horse race. It has been renewed annually without interruption since that first running in 1875, is America's oldest continually-held sports event and the first race in the internationally renowned "Triple Crown" series of races. Clark's track was located on property owned by his uncles, John and Henry Churchill, and it came to be known within a few years as Churchill Downs.

The track's original clubhouse and grandstand were replaced in 1895 with a new grandstand topped by a distinctive architectural flourish, a pair of structures that have come to be known worldwide as the "Twin Spires." Those spires remain Churchill Downs' most recognizable feature and are the epitome of the now commonplace practice of "branding" a signature design element for advertising purposes. A clubhouse was added to the track when a new ownership team headed by Louisville businessman Matt J. Winn purchased the then-struggling Churchill Downs in 1902. Winn revitalized both the Kentucky Derby

and the track, which underwent significant expansions in the 1920s, the 1960s and again in 2003-'04. The Kentucky Derby, which is run each year on the first Saturday in May, has also been dubbed the "Run for the Roses" and "the greatest two minutes in sports." The race is preceded by the bugler's traditional "Call to the Post," and the singing of Stephen Foster's "My Old Kentucky Home." Both are part of a proud tradition that is deeply revered by local residents and visitors alike. The Derby has been preceded since 1956 by the Kentucky Derby Festival, which has grown into a two-week-long celebration of locally-supported activities and events.

Churchill Downs was designated as a National Historic Landmark in 1986, an honor that recognized the role the racetrack had played in the horse racing industry in the state and nation and the status of the Kentucky Derby as one of America's greatest sporting events.

Formerly the location of the Offices of the Mayor and 12-member Board of Aldermen, City Hall today houses the offices of the 26 members of Louisville's Metro Council.

LOUISVILLE CITY HALL

Location/Address:	601 West Jefferson Street
Dates:	1870-1873
Style:	Italianate/Second Empire
Architects/Builders:	City Hall by John Andrewartha (1870-73); Clock tower by Henry Whitestone (1876)
Historic Status:	Metro Landmark, National Register of Historic Places

City Hall, an Italianate and Second Empire monolith, is perhaps the most fanciful public building in the Louisville metro area. Three stories in height, its massing, hallmarked by distinct façade planes that project and recess in an undulating fashion, add interest to the building's architectural composition. The building's clock tower addresses its corner site. Because the clock itself is a functional feature, it is a landmark that citizens can literally set their watches to. However, it is the stone carving that sets this building apart from other civic structures. Louisville's early agricultural history is referenced by the sculpted heads of pigs, cows, and horses proudly displayed above the windows on the second story. The pediment over the building's main entrance, symbolically expresses the progressive optimism of post Civil War Louisville: a relief sculpture depicts a northern train bearing the word "progress" plowing south through the forest toward a palm tree.

John Andrewartha conceived and executed the building's original design, while Henry Whitestone was responsible for City Halls' clock tower. Andrewatha was born and received his early training in England. He arrived in Louisville in 1865 and immediately gained a reputation as a favored architect to the city's elite, and was known for his flamboyant designs. In addition to numerous residences, Andrewartha designed the Central Colored School, the City Almshouse, and Louisville's Eruptive Hospital. Henry Whitestone was born and educated in Ireland. He immigrated to the United States with his family in 1852. Whitestone was associated with famed hotel architect Isaiah Rogers, and is credited with the design of many of Louisville's finest residences and businesses. Louisville's City Hall has the distinction of being the largest extant example of the Italianate style and is even more unusual because of its Second Empire stylistic overtones.

CLIFTON DISTRICT

Location/Address:	East of downtown, sandwiched between the Butchertown and Crescent Hill neighborhoods
Dates:	1860s to 1950s
Style:	Late Victorian Eclectic Styles (Italianate, Queen Anne, Princess Anne, Tudor, Gothic Revival), and Craftsman Bungalow style
Architects/Builders:	Multiple
Historic Status:	Metro Landmark District, National Register of Historic Places

The Clifton neighborhood is composed of 423 acres and is bounded by Brownsboro Road, Interstate 64, Ewing Avenue, and Mellwood Avenue. It derives its name from one of the area's most important landholders, gentleman farmer Colonel Joshua B. Bowles, who built an estate called Clifton near what is now the corner of Vernon and Sycamore Avenues between 1817 and 1842.

As the Louisville and Shelbyville Turnpike and the Louisville and Frankfort Railroad made the areas east of downtown more accessible, an increasing number of people moved out to the countryside. By the mid-1800s emerging industries began to attract residents to the area. The constant water supply provided by the Middle Fork of Beargrass Creek brought distilling and the slaughtering and processing of meats to areas nearby, while an abundance of limestone attracted quarrymen who slowly carved away huge chunks of hillside. While some subdivision of land occurred as early as the 1850s, it was not until after the Civil War that it was in full swing. The western tip of Clifton was annexed by Louisville in 1856. In 1867, with a population of 75, a group of civic-minded residents successfully petitioned the state legislature to grant a charter to the town of Clifton. It was engulfed by subsequent annexations that occurred in 1895 and 1897. With time, a mature, mixed-use neighborhood emerged that was largely late Victorian in design. Modest one- and two-story frame and brick houses lined the side streets, with Frankfort Avenue serving as the primary commercial core.

Remnants of Clifton's historic past have served the neighborhood well. Residential building styles reflect the architectural fashions popular between 1880 and 1910, the area's major period of development, and include buildings

Frankfort Avenue (shown above circa 1940s) is Clifton's main business corridor, and today includes revitalized homes, restaurants, and small businesses. The Clifton Market (left), shown in 1883, is still in business today on Frankfort Avenue.

in the Italianate, Queen Anne, Princess Anne, Tudor, Gothic Revival, and Craftsman Bungalow styles. With the popularization of the automobile and the extension of city street car lines, the Frankfort Avenue corridor began to take on a "layered" effect, with newer storefronts added onto older residential and commercial buildings.

The neighborhood has felt resurgence in recent years as people rediscover its unique historic character, and younger people have moved there to remodel the wide variety of houses. Neighborhood groups such as the Clifton Community Council and the Frankfort Avenue Business Association have bolstered community pride as well. A wide variety of new businesses have sprung up along Frankfort Avenue, especially restaurants. In 2003, Clifton became a designated historic preservation district.

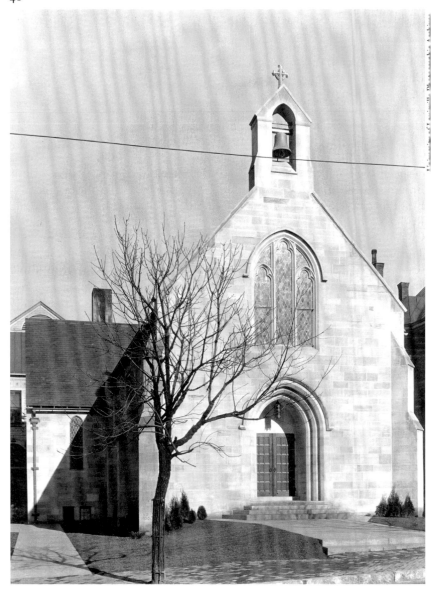

CONCORDIA LUTHERAN CHURCH

Location/Address:	1127 East Broadway
Date:	1930
Style:	Gothic Revival
Architect/Builder:	Ralph Adams Cram
Historic Status:	National Register of Historic Places

One of the nation's foremost church architects, Ralph Adams Cram, designed this delightful Gothic Revival style building on prominent East Broadway in the early 1900s. Nestled in the heart of the Highlands on busy East Broadway, Cram executed a small-scale "jewel box" church in the Gothic Revival style. It is both refined and understated. All of the usual trappings of Gothic Revival style are employed, but in a simplified and refined manner. The diminutive Concordia Lutheran Church is one of a rare group of small-scale churches designed by Cram, distinguished ecclesiastical architect and leading proponent of the English Gothic Revival style in America. Cram also designed the U.S. Military Academy at West Point, New York, and St. John the Divine in New York City, a building widely regarded as his architectural masterpiece. As supervising architect he also designed buildings at Princeton University, Bryn Mawr, Mount Holyoke, and Wellesley Colleges. Charles J. Connick Associates of Boston produced the stained-glass windows.

COUNTRY ESTATES OF RIVER ROAD

Location/Address:	Along River Road between Longview Lane to just east of U.S. Highway 42
Dates:	1875-1938, with most constructed between 1905-1916
Style:	Multiple
Architects/Builders:	Multiple; many were architect-designed, some estates were built to include designed historic landscape elements
Historic Status:	National Register of Historic Places

A narrow gauge railroad, and later an interurban rail route, facilitated the development of a series of Country Estates located along River Road and its side streets. Many were perched on high river bluffs that afforded their wealthy owners expansive views of the scenic Ohio River below. These country estates were built by Louisville's owner-manager class as year-round retreats for themselves and their families. They were intended to provide relief from the daily hustle and bustle of city life. Ownership patterns represent a veritable "Who's Who" of Louisville with many of the city's wealthiest citizens building estates in this area. Together, the Country Estates represent an astounding architectural and cultural landscape legacy. Although some houses date from as early as 1875, most were constructed between 1905 and 1916, in direct correlation to easy access to the interurban rail line that paralleled River Road. Not only are most of the houses high-style, architect-designed masterpieces, many authored by well-known, out-of-town architects, but also a high number had professionally designed formal and informal landscapes surrounding their property as well. Frederick Law Olmsted and his successor firms were responsible for many. The majority of houses in the Country Estates area are not accessible to the public or even visible from the public right-of-way. However, Glenview Station, a former rail station for the Louisville, Harrods Creek, and Westport Railroad and later an interurban station, is open to the public. Although interurban rail service ended in 1935, this building has housed a branch of the Glenview Post Office since 1898.

Between 1841 and 1880, the year the tavern closed, the tavern was a focal point of Middletown's agriculture and commercial activities. It will be rehabilitated as Middletown's City Hall.

Davis Tavern/Middletown City Hall

Location/Address:	11180 Old Shelbyville Road
Dates:	Constructed circa 1797; enlarged, 1841; Tudor porch added late 19th century
Style:	Federal I-House with Gothic Revival porch addition
Architect/Builder:	William White, owner
Historic Status:	City of Middletown Local Preservation District
	National Register of Historic Places

     The Davis Tavern is a two-story, brick, Federal-style I-house constructed in 1796 for William White, an early settler of Middletown. White, who came to Kentucky from Westmoreland County, Virginia, was a municipal trustee and authored Middletown's first town plan in 1797. He built the original five-bay section as his residence. After White's death, his son-in-law, Lawrence Young, took possession of the house and surrounding farmland and may have operated a school in the building at that time. In 1841, the property was sold to Susan B. Davis, a White heir. Soon after, the building was converted to the Davis Tavern, and three additional bays were added. A one-story porch with Tudor arches and octagonal support posts that rest upon a brush-hammered limestone base was added sometime in the late 19th century and is perhaps the building's most identifiable feature. At some point, portions of the brick building were stuccoed. Davis Tavern is an important and rare early structure that typifies building styles locally popular during the late-18th through the mid-19th centuries. A pair of cut limestone gateposts that once served to mark the entrance to a now-demolished stable are a reminder of the building's days as a stagecoach stop. Davis Tavern was strategically sited on Main Street in Middletown (the old Shelbyville Turnpike) a vital east-west transportation conduit.

ANTON AND J.W. DIEBOLD HOUSES

Location/Address:	4119 West Broadway and 4303 West Broadway
Dates:	Anton Diebold house built 1911-12; J.W. Diebold house built 1913
Style:	Classical Revival
Architects/Builders:	Architect, unknown; John Diebold and Sons, builder

In 1911, Anton Diebold began construction of this grand residence on West Broadway. Two years later John Diebold Jr. built a house on the same street two blocks from Anton. Both worked for the John Diebold and Sons Stone Company, a cut stone contracting company, and both faced their residences in this durable material. One of their most prominent commissions was the stonework of the Beaux-Arts style City Hall Annex built in 1907-09 adjacent to City Hall. What sets these two residences apart from their neighbors is their superb stone carvings and craftsmanship. The John Diebold House features ashlar stone laid in alternating broad and narrow horizontal bands. Stone steps lead up to a recessed porch lined with smooth stone columns supporting a full entablature. The Anton Diebold House, by contrast, takes on a Greek Temple form with a main façade that features a columned portico topped by Corinthian columns.

The Anton Diebold House (above), at 4303 West Broadway, and the John Diebold house (right) at 4119 West Broadway, are fine examples of grand residential construction once popular in the city's west end.

The Squire Earick House was built sometime between 1811 and 1827 in Louisville's Portland neighborhood.

EARICK HOUSE

\Location/address:	719 North 34th Street
Dates:	Circa 1811-1827
Style:	Federal
Architect/Builder:	Unknown
Historic Status:	National Register of Historic Places

One of the area's oldest examples of frame construction, the two-story, timber frame Squire Earick House is an important remnant of Louisville's early settlement period. A broad, recessed one-story porch spans the width of the building's north façade and is topped by a second story above. On the interior, single large rooms flank a central hall and stairway. Each room has a chimney and fireplace in its gable end. Intricately detailed woodwork and discreetly placed end cabinets in extant Federal mantels show a high level of craftsmanship. Also of note are the banister and newel post that are identical to plans published as early as 1806 in the first edition of Asher Benjamin's "The American Builder's Companion or a New System of Architecture." Curiously, archaeological investigations conducted for the Portland Museum reveal that the foundation of the house may not be as old as the house itself. This leads to speculation that an older house may have been moved to the present foundation from a nearby location. Furthermore, there is evidence suggesting that a timber frame kitchen addition was turned 180 degrees and attached to the present structure. Additionally, the south side of the house exhibits as many as three distinct building phases.

The house's rich history, now most closely associated with Portland's first magistrate, Squire Jacob Earick, reflects Portland's role as an independent river town at the Falls of the Ohio. Ownership records reveal that several families important to Kentucky and Portland history have owned the property. These include General William Lytle, Robert Todd, R.S., Allen Campbell, and David Shields. When Magistrate Earick resided in this house, it is reported that he held court on the dining room table and held prisoners in the cellar. Additional research, assisted in part by the Save America's Treasures program of the National Park Service, is shedding more light on the rich and colorful history of this intriguing house and its occupants and will underpin its restoration and interpretation.

FARMINGTON

Location/Address:	3033 Bardstown Road
Dates:	1815-1816
Style:	Federal
Architects/Builders:	Paul Skidmore, architect/Robert Nicholson, master carpenter. There is some evidence to link the design of Farmington to Thomas Jefferson.
Historic Status:	National Register of Historic Places.

Farmington, the centerpiece of a 550-acre hemp plantation, was the home of John Speed and Lucy Gilmer Fry Speed, their family, and up to 60 enslaved African Americans. The 14-room Federal-style house dates from 1815-1816. An original building contract, discovered in 1998, identifies Robert Nicholson as the master carpenter and Paul Skidmore as the person who drew up the plans for the house. Circumstantial evidence suggests that the design may have been based on plans conceived by Thomas Jefferson. Lucy Speed's family had close connections to Jefferson. Her grandfather served as his guardian for a time and her uncle and aunt lived at Farmington in Charlottesville, Virginia, a house with a documented Jefferson addition for which the Louisville Farmington was named. Farmington's unusual plan with its two central octagonal rooms and suppressed staircases bears close similarities to an existing Jefferson plan for an unknown house. Also of note at Farmington is the Speed family connection to Abraham Lincoln who visited Farmington for three weeks in 1841.

Joshua Speed, son of John Speed, shared a room with Lincoln in Springfield, Illinois for nearly three years and is said by scholars to have been Lincoln's closest friend. James Speed, Joshua's brother, served as Attorney General in Lincoln's last cabinet, staying on after the president's assassination. Historic Homes Foundation Inc. was formed in 1957 to acquire Farmington, which opened as a museum in 1959. The foundation is chartered to purchase, preserve and display historic sites and to advance education, culture and the arts in Kentucky. Today, Farmington remains the flagship of the Historic Homes Foundation and Louisville's first historic house museum. It was documented by the Historic American Buildings Survey in 1934 and is one of the Louisville area's earliest listings in the National Register of Historic Places.

52

Borb photos University of Louisville Photographic Archives

The Kentucky State Fair Board Merchants and Manufacturing Building was used as a state fairground until replacement by the larger Kentucky Fair and Exposition Center in south Louisville in 1956.

KENTUCKY STATE FAIR BOARD MERCHANTS AND MANUFACTURING BUILDING

Location/Address:	1400 South 43rd Street (at Rankin Avenue)
Date:	1921
Style:	Spanish Renaissance Revival
Architect/Builder:	Joseph & Joseph
Historic Status:	National Register of Historic Places

.

In 1921 the local architectural firm of Joseph & Joseph completed work on the Merchants and Manufacturering Building for the Kentucky State Fair. It is one of Louisville's largest and most impressive examples of Spanish Renaissance style architecture. The Kentucky State Fair Board Merchants and Manufacturing Building was built to showcase the state's yearly celebration of economic progress and cultural activity based on agriculture. It is three stories in height and is clad in stucco. The two-story, centered, multi-bay entrance is topped by a Baroque-style parapet wall. Three-story square end towers capped by cupolas with domed roofs, in turn, flank it.

Upon its completion it was touted as the largest structure of its kind in the world, reportedly surpassing Madison Square Garden in size. Remarkably, five railroad cars of tile, seven thousand square feet of skylights and one ton of galvanized sheets of roofing were used in its construction. The building's interior features a large open exhibit space with clerestory windows that allow for a well-lit interior. Steel truss work is visibly expressed on the building's interior roof structure.

Fire Station Number Two/ Sinking Fund Building

Location/Address:	619 West Jefferson Street
Date:	1891
Style:	Richardsonian Romanesque
Architect/Builder:	McDonald Brothers, architects
Historic Status:	Select historic firehouses are Louisville Metro Landmarks; many are listed in the National Register of Historic Places

Fire Station Number Two harks back to the golden age of firefighting in Louisville. In the city's formative years, fires were fought by volunteers. By 1858, a professional fire department was established. Over time, the city developed a highly respected and sophisticated firefighting team using the most advanced equipment that included steam engines, chemical engines and hook-and-ladders. Neighborhood fire stations were often points of civic pride, designed by the city's most prominent local architects. Fire Station Number Two was constructed in 1891 based on a design by the McDonald Brothers, a local architectural firm. It is the epitome of the Richardsonian Romanesque style. The strength conveyed through its architecture is quite appropriate for this utilitarian building. Announcing the building's role as the chief fire station for Louisville was the ribbed domical belfry from which firemen were called into service. While the tower base remains, the belfry itself has been removed. As with City Hall, the language of architecture, through the building's carved detailing, is used to symbolically convey its function. Firemen's helmets and entwined fire hoses are featured just above the spring of two of the building's three ground-level Richardsonian Romanesque arches while profiles of two locally prominent fire chiefs are situated within two of the building's front facing pediments. While Louisville has numerous excellent examples of buildings in the Richardsonian Romanesque style, this structure is without question the finest civic expression of the style.

The McDonald Brothers, Harry P. and Kenneth, were best known for their designs of public buildings across the south. Among the styles they favored were the Victorian Gothic and Beaux-Arts. However, they also designed numerous factories, office buildings, and civic structures in these styles as well.

BENJAMIN I. HEAD HOUSE

Location/Address: 11601 Main Street
Dates: Circa 1813-1815
Style: Federal
Architect/Builder: Benjamin I. Head
Historic Status: City of Middletown Local Preservation District
                      National Register of Historic Places

Benjamin I. Head was a Revolutionary War captain, early settler to the area, Middletown trustee, and local businessman. He built this two-story, Federal-style side hall plan residence of cut stone between 1813 and 1815. Its construction occurred simultaneously with the erection of an adjacent (but now demolished) stone commercial building that served as the Head, Hobbs, and Lawrence General Store. The store attracted a steady clientele who depended on Head, Hobbs, and Lawrence for merchandise purchased and transported by horseback from as far east as Philadelphia and Baltimore. By 1820, after accumulation of gambling debts, Head relocated to a nearby farm. Shortly after the Civil War it was sold to Silas Witherbee, first president of the Bank of Middletown, and magistrate for eastern Jefferson County.

Constructed of twenty-two inch thick walls of hand-cut limestone, the Head House features a sophisticated, three-bay, asymmetrical building front. Its most striking architectural feature is the entryway composed of a double door flanked by sidelights and topped by a delicate elliptical fanlight. Nine-over-six light windows balance this façade arrangement. Stone chimneys top the building.

Today the Head House and outbuildings house a collection of antique and gift shops.

The Head House, shown here in a circa-1890 photograph, served as a general store in the early 19th century, and nearly 190 years later is still part of the commercial life of Middletown.

HUMANA TOWER

Location/Address:	500 West Main Street
Date:	1985
Style:	Post-Modern
Architect/Builder:	Michael Graves

The Humana Tower is a 27-story, post-modern style building designed by architect Michael Graves and built between 1982-1985. The Graves design was the result of a design competition hosted by the Louisville-based health care giant Humana, Inc. The building serves as Humana's corporate headquarters. The Graves design prevailed over designs by notable internationally-recognized architects Cesar Pelli, Norman Foster, Ulrich Franzen, and Helmut Jahn. Graves, a professor of architecture at Princeton University, designed a columned loggia on the lower level that reflects the small-scale, commercial, cast-iron buildings along Main Street. The top features a truss assembly reminiscent of Ohio River bridges. The tinted green shaft of glass on the primary façade resembles a waterfall. While the initial reaction to the design of the Humana building was mixed, it spawned a host of similarly-styled buildings and is widely regarded as the inspiration for the post-modern movement in architecture worldwide.

JEFFERSON COUNTY COURTHOUSE/
LOUISVILLE METRO HALL

Location/Address:	527 West Jefferson Street
Dates:	1835-60
Style:	Greek Revival
Architects/Builders:	Designed by Gideon Shryock (1835); modified by Albert Fink 1858-60); Brinton B. Davis (1905)
Historic Status:	Metro Landmark, National Register of Historic Places

The Jefferson County Courthouse has been referred to as one of the major surviving monuments to Greek Revival style architecture in America. Indeed, Marcus Whiffin, author of *American Architecture Since 1780* cites the architect of the building, Gideon Shryock, as being "of more than local importance." The building displays all of the hallmarks of the Greek Revival style: block-like massing, symmetry, smooth wall surfaces, low pitch to the roof, trabeated construction, and the like. But perhaps the building's most dominant, character-defining feature is the entrance portico with colossal columns, strong/substantial entablature, and prominent pediment. This building holds the distinction of being the oldest extant civic building in Louisville and is, without question, the area's finest civic expression of Greek Revival style architecture. Gideon Shryock, engaged as a city architect by both city and county governments as a joint commission, designed and constructed the building. Among Shryock's other noteworthy buildings are the Old State Capitol Building in Frankfort, Kentucky, the Morrison College Building in Lexington, Kentucky, and the Old State Capitol Building in Little Rock, Arkansas.

Difficulties encountered by Shryock while overseeing construction of the courthouse caused his dismissal as city architect in 1842, and he never again received a major local architectural commission. He died in obscurity in 1874. Engineer Albert Fink replaced Shryock. German-born and trained, Fink was best known as a capable engineer and bridge designer. Fink's training as an engineer is reflected in the Jefferson County Courthouse's use of cast iron, particularly on the floor of the building's rotunda.

The Jefferson County Courthouse now serves as Louisville Metro Hall, offices of the Mayor of Louisville Metro and the Jefferson County Clerk.

Use of the Jefferson County Jail building as a jail has been discontinued but it is still owned by local government and now houses state and municipal offices.

JEFFERSON COUNTY JAIL

Location/Address:	514 West Liberty Street
Dates:	1902-05
Style:	Romanesque Revival
Architects/Builders:	D.X. Murphy and Brothers
Historic Status:	Metro Landmark, National Register of Historic Places

The Old Jail, designed by D. X. Murphy, was built in 1905. It bears a resemblance to Burnham and Root's famous Chicago landmark, the Monadnock Building. It consists of two blocks architecturally unified by a recessed brick hyphen. The east block was originally the administrative wing while the west block was the original cellblock for prisoners. The language of architecture was used here to convey a message: the administrative wing, as originally constructed, is clearly accessible to the public with a series of steps that lead to a raised first floor level, while the fortress-like cellblock appeared "impenetrable" because it was built with no visible entrance. Upon completion it was considered one of the most modern correctional facilities in the country because it reflected the latest trends in sanitation, security, and mechanics. Two hundred forty cells had a remarkably innovative locking system that allowed guards the choice of opening one cell or all cells on each tier.

KADEN TOWER/LINCOLN TOWER/ LINCOLN INCOME LIFE INSURANCE COMPANY BUILDING

Location/Address: 6100 Dutchmans Lane
Date: 1965
Style: Modern
Architect/Builder: William Wesley Peters

      Kaden Tower, a St. Matthews-area landmark, was constructed in 1965 based on a design by William Wesley Peters, a protégé and student of famed architect Frank Lloyd Wright. It was constructed to house a life insurance company but now serves as general office space. Its innovative and unusual appearance can be attributed to the fact that Kaden Tower was constructed with a load bearing central utility core from which the 15 floors of the building hang in a cantilevered fashion. Concrete panels with a lace-like motif serve as the building's exterior slipcover. Functional as well as practical, the lightweight panels cut down on the infiltration of direct sunlight (and correspondingly reduce cooling costs) while permitting those inside the building to enjoy breathtaking views of the surrounding area.

KAUFMAN-STRAUS BUILDING

Location/Address:	533-49 Fourth Street
Date:	1903
Style:	Chicago School
Architect/Builder:	Mason Maury
Historic Status:	National Register of Historic Places

Influential local architect Mason Maury (1846-1919) won a design competition for the six-story Kaufman-Straus Building. The building's owner, the Polytechnic Society (precursor to the Louisville Free Public Library) hosted the competition. It is one of Louisville's best examples of the Chicago School of Architecture. The Kaufman-Straus Building is stylistically reminiscent of Louis Sullivan's 1898 Gage Building in Chicago. It was designed to serve as a department store on the lower floors with a library on the top, and is a notable local example of an early mixed-use commercial building. It is constructed of brick and terra cotta. In the Chicago School tradition, the building's façade is horizontally separated into base, shaft and capital. Uninterrupted pilasters that create distinct divisions for each of the building's five bays further articulate it vertically. Each pilaster is topped by an ornate foliate design reminiscent of Sullivan's work (*see above*). More slender minor pilasters located between each major pilaster further divide each bay in half again. A prominent cornice tops the building. The Kaufman-Straus Building now forms the eastern wall of the *Fourth Street Live!* entertainment complex at Fourth Street between Muhammad Ali Boulevard and Liberty Street.

KENTUCKY HOME LIFE BUILDING

Location/Address:	239-47 West Jefferson Street
Dates:	1913, 1922
Style:	Chicago School with Beaux-Arts details
Architects/Builders:	Brinton B. Davis (1913); addition by D.X. Murphy (1922)
Historic Status:	National Register of Historic Places

The Inter-Southern Life Insurance Company Building is a 20-story downtown office building constructed in 1913. For many years it was considered one of the most prestigious business addresses in downtown Louisville because of its location at the heart of the city's financial and judicial center. Up until 1955 it was the tallest building in the city. Designed by prominent local architect Brinton B. Davis, it follows the Chicago School architectural formula of base, column, and shaft. Reportedly, it was one of Davis' most important commissions and garnered him much attention. The architect went on to design the Jefferson County Armory/Louisville Gardens, the Parkland Branch Library, and the Ashley Hotel in Atlanta. As originally constructed, the Inter-Southern Life Insurance Building housed a bank on the first floor and the Inter-Southern Life Insurance Company, its major occupant, on the entire lower floor. On the remaining floors there was space for up to 300 additional offices. In 1922 another local architect, D.X. Murphy, designed an addition that mimicked the original. Its most striking feature is the ground-level banking room designed to replicate the Roman Baths of Caracalla. The room is three stories high, features fluted Corinthian columns supporting a broad entablature, and is topped by a coffered, barrel-vaulted ceiling pierced by lunettes with windows. Murphy also designed the St. Boniface Church and rectory, the old Jefferson County Jail, and the former German Bank Building. When sold in 1932, the building's name was changed from the Inter-Southern Life Insurance Building to the Kentucky Home Life Building, a name that has carried through to the present day.

78255

INTER-SOUTHERN BLDG.

PHOTO BY CAUFIELD AND SHOOK

LEVY BROTHERS BUILDING

Location/Address:	235 West Market Street
Date:	1893
Style:	Richardsonian Romanesque
Architects/Builders:	Charles J. Clarke and Arthur Loomis
Historic Status:	National Register of Historic Places

German émigré brothers Henry and Moses Levy built the Levy Brothers Building in 1893 as a men's clothing store. The brothers had begun their career in retail as itinerant peddlers but eventually settled in Louisville around 1861. When the first store no longer held sufficient space for their growing business they built the present building on West Market Street. It is an excellent example of the Richardsonian Romanesque style of architecture and was designed by Charles J. Clarke and Arthur Loomis, two prominent local architects. In 1908, as a publicity ploy, the building's windows were outlined in lights. As a result, the phrase "lit up like Levy's" was used locally to refer to someone who had either had a bit too much to drink or to a building that had been illuminated in a gaudy fashion. Growth in the retail clothing business eventually led to the construction of four stores in suburban locations. Because of an economic downturn for retailers in Louisville's Central Business District, the clothing retailer closed up shop in 1979 after 118 years on Market Street. Closure of their suburban stores followed soon after. The building now serves as a mixed-use structure with a restaurant on the ground level and offices and apartments on the upper floors. It was one of the city's early Investment Tax Credit projects.

LIMERICK DISTRICT

Location/Address:	South of Louisville's Central Business District and north of Old Louisville, bounded by Breckinridge Street, Oak Street, the old Louisville and Nashville railroad tracks and Ninth and Fifth Streets
Dates:	1860s-1910s
Style:	Late Victorian Eclectic (Queen Anne, Princess Anne, Richardsonian Romanesque, Italianate, Tudor, Classical Revival and Craftsman)
Architect/Builder:	Multiple
Historic Status:	Metro Landmark District, National Register of Historic Places

Limerick developed as an enclave for Irish immigrants beginning in about 1860. Many sought employment at the old Louisville and Nashville Railroad repair shops, freight yard, and depot in the area. In 1869, the name Limerick was officially adopted at a meeting held at the predominantly Irish St. Louis Bertrand Catholic Church that was called expressly to decide how the developing area was to be named. In the early years, Limerick was modest. Later in the century, as the economic base of the community improved, smaller dwellings were replaced with more substantial ones. The variety of economic incomes, occupations and ethnic backgrounds over several distinct spurts of development has resulted in a patchwork of housing types and styles, including Queen Anne, Princess Anne, Richardsonian Romanesque, Italianate, Tudor, Classical Revival and Craftsman. Many in Limerick occupied large Victorian dwellings on the major streets while African Americans, by and large, lived along the alleys on minor streets in shotgun houses. The high number of African Americans, many of whom had lived in the area before the Civil War and were employed as slaves or servants, warranted the construction of the Central Colored School in 1873 at Fifth and Kentucky Streets. It was the first tax-supported public school for African Americans in the state. Designed by local architect John B. McElfatrick, the three-story brick structure was later re-named the Mary D. Hill School. In 1879, the General Association of Colored Baptists in Kentucky opened Simmons University. It was the first institution of higher education in Kentucky that was controlled by African Americans.

In 1884, it was known as the State University and in 1920 it was renamed Simmons University to honor William Simmons, former president of the school. African American architect and contractor Samuel Plato, a former student of the institution, designed a "dormitory for boys" (now Steward Hall) on campus. In 1930, it became known as the Municipal College for Negroes and was affiliated with the University of Louisville until closure in 1951 with the end of educational desegregation. In 1905, when L&N's repair shops moved south and its presence in Limerick ended, the neighborhood began to take on a new character. The more affluent Irish moved away to more fashionable areas of the city. As whites moved out, African Americans moved out of alley structures to take up residence in the larger houses on Limerick's major streets. In recent years, the number of renovations in the area has escalated as the adjacent Old Louisville neighborhood to the south has become more popular.

LOCUST GROVE

Location/Address:	561 Blankenbaker Lane
Date:	Circa 1790
Style:	Georgian
Architects/Builders:	Major William Croghan, owner; Walter M. Macomber, circa 1960s restoration architect in association with Nevin and Morgan
Historic Status:	National Historic Landmark, Metro Landmark, National Register of Historic Places

Locust Grove, built circa 1790 by William Croghan, is the only extant structure in Kentucky associated with the Lewis and Clark Expedition. It is a twelve-room, two-and-a-half-story, double pile, Georgian house. It was originally the focal point of a 694-acre farm, of which 55 acres remain intact today. Formal gardens, a stone wall, and several outbuildings dot the historic landscape. Lucy Clark Croghan, wife of William, was a sister of William Clark of the famed Lewis and Clark expedition. In 1806 Meriwether Lewis and Clark stopped at Locust Grove on their way back from the Pacific.

Founder of Louisville and Revolutionary War hero General George Rogers Clark, another of Lucy's brothers, spent his last years at Locust Grove and died there in 1818. Other dignitaries to visit Locust Grove include former Vice President Aaron Burr, President James Monroe, General Andrew Jackson (who would later become the 17th United States president), artist and naturalist John James Audubon, and noted abolitionist Cassius Marcellus Clay.

Collections in the house, which include several pieces once owned by Clark and Croghan, represent the period from 1760 to 1840.

In 1961, when the house was to be sold at auction, the Commonwealth of Kentucky and Jefferson County purchased the property to ensure its preservation. Restoration began soon after and the house opened for tours in 1964. For many years, Locust Grove was managed by the Historic Homes Foundation on behalf of Jefferson County, under a joint agreement between the Commonwealth of Kentucky and the county.

Locust Grove has two important facades—the front (above), and rear (below) which features a wide and inviting gallery.

Both photos by Louisville Metro Planning and Design

◼ LOEW'S THEATER/UNITED ARTISTS THEATER ◼
THE LOUISVILLE PALACE THEATRE

Location/Address:	625 South Fourth Street
Dates:	1928, 1981
Style:	Spanish Baroque Atmospheric
Architect/Builder:	John Eberson
Historic Status:	National Register of Historic Places

The grandest of Louisville's movie houses is the Palace Theatre. The theater was originally known as Loew's Theater (1928) but later underwent numerous name changes including: Loew's United Artist Theater (1948); United Artist Theater (mid-1950s); United Artists/Penthouse Theater (1963); and finally, the Louisville Palace (1978-79). This 3,300-seat building was designed as a silent film house but was later converted to a movie theater. It first served as the local film outlet for both Metro-Goldwin-Mayer and Columbia. First-run films were a hallmark. Its premiere in 1929 featured the films "Excess Baggage" and "The Old Gray Horse." Architect John Eberson, American movie palace design pioneer, conceived this "atmospheric" theater as he did nearly one hundred others across the nation. Under the Eberson concept, moviegoers were transported to another place and time through the creative use of exotic architecture. Louisville's Loew's Theater is considered one of his most unusual. The multi-story exterior of Loew's Theater is faced with vibrantly glazed and highly textured architectural terra cotta and completed with a marquee. On the building's interior, escapism is at an all time high where the lobby design includes a barrel vaulted, coffered "ceiling of celebrities" featuring 130 historical figures in plaster bas relief. The main theater space takes on the atmosphere of

a Spanish garden at night. Statues are set in intricately-detailed plaster niches on walls with surface ornamentation too intricate to describe in detail. A twinkling night sky mimicking a star pattern is created by a multitude of tiny, blinking lights. The "cloud machine" that projected an image of clouds appearing to move slowly across the night sky is no longer in operation. A screaming macaw, symbol of Loew's theaters, was perched in the lobby on opening night in 1928. Every silent-film house of the day featured an organ and Loew's was no exception. At the beginning of each film, a spotlit Wurlitzer organ would dramatically rise by mechanical lift 15 feet above the stage.

Businessman John Siegel beautifully restored the building in 1981. It now features a wide variety of traveling theatrical productions, Broadway-style shows, entertainers and an occasional movie.

LOUISVILLE MUNICIPAL (SECOND STREET) BRIDGE

Location/Address:	Second and Main Streets
Date:	1929
Style:	Moderne
Architects/Builders:	Modjeski and Masters, engineers; Paul Phillipe Cret, architect; Contractors included American Bridge Company, the Vang Construction Company, and the Henry Bickel Company
Historic Status:	National Register of Historic Places

The construction of the Louisville Municipal Bridge represents an important chapter in Louisville and southern Indiana's architectural, engineering, and transportation history. Widely recognized as an engineering milestone in bridge construction, the 3,740-foot-long Louisville Municipal Bridge was the first highway bridge constructed across the Ohio River. President Herbert Hoover dedicated it during the same week as the Stock Market Crash of 1929. Owned by the City of Louisville and serving as a toll bridge until 1949 (the year it was renamed in honor of Louisville's founder George Rogers Clark), the Clark Memorial Bridge now is owned and maintained by the Commonwealth of Kentucky.

The Municipal Bridge is best described as a single-deck, six-span cantilevered truss bridge with Warren through trusses. It has smooth-faced limestone pylons on each shore that are adorned with an engaged fluted column emblazoned with a sculptured eagle and topped by a bronze lantern. Each bears the name and symbol of its respective state. Due to land acquisition delays, bridge construction actually commenced not on either shoreline, but at mid-river using a method dubbed the "guy derrick system." Derricks were attached to the main tower piers with structural systems suspended from them in a modular, cantilevered fashion. As each section was completed, the derricks were moved to the next section needing completion. The American Bridge Company, under contract with the engineering firm of Modjeski and Masters, conceived this engineering concept (Modjeski and Masters also designed the Huey P. Long Bridge and the San Francisco-Oakland Bay Bridge). Both sets of pylons on the Kentucky and Indiana approaches to the bridge as well as the administration building located

This view of the Louisville Municipal (Second Street) Bridge from the 1930s was taken from the corner of Second and Main on the Louisville side of the Ohio River.

in Jeffersonville, Indiana are rare local examples of the Moderne style and are the work of Ecole des Beaux Arts-trained, world-renowned architect and educator Paul Phillipe Cret. The French-born Cret was also responsible for the design of the Integrity Trust Building (1929); the Rodin Museum (1932) and the Federal Reserve Building both in Philadelphia; and the Folger Shakespeare Memorial Library (1932) in Washington, D.C. As a Professor of Design in the School of Architecture at the University of Pennsylvania, he trained Louis I. Kahn (1901-1974), his most famous student.

■ Louisville War Memorial Auditorium ■

Location/Address:	970 South Fourth Street
Dates:	1927-29
Style:	Beaux-Arts Classicism
Architects/Builders:	Thomas Hastings (of Carrere and Hastings), in association with E. T. Hutchings
Historic Status:	Metro Landmark, National Register of Historic Places

Built to honor the soldiers, sailors and marines from Jefferson County who gave their lives during World War I, this auditorium was dedicated on Memorial Day, 1929. It satisfied both the local need for assembly space and the desire to honor war dead. Thomas Hastings of the New York architectural firm of Carrere and Hastings designed it, in association with the local firm of E.T. Hutchings. Among other works by Carrere and Hastings are the New York Central Public Library and the Senate Office Buildings in Washington, D.C. The building's symmetrical façade, which is faced in coursed ashlar limestone masonry with a rubbed finish, features a colossal Doric order portico topped by a full entablature. Bas-relief carved ornamentation is prevalent. A dome, said to be larger in diameter than the Pantheon in Rome, tops the building's main auditorium space. On an upper floor, the Flag Room features mahogany cases containing a display of flags of many nations assembled in the 1920s by the Society for the Perpetual Observance of Armistice Day. Buried in Memorial Auditorium's cornerstone, among other artifacts and relics, is a list of men and women from Jefferson County who sacrificed their lives; a photograph of Woodrow Wilson, war president; a copy of the Congressional proclamation declaring war with Germany; and a history of the Jefferson County Chapter of the American War Mothers.

LUSTRON HOMES

Lustron is the trade name for a one-story, prefabricated, maintenance-free, metal ranch house developed in the 1940s by Chicago industrial engineer, Carl Strandlund (designer of Standard Oil gas stations). Former Mayor of Louisville Wilson Wyatt played a major role in its development when he, as National Housing Expediter under the Harry Truman administration (1945-1953), agreed to allocate steel for its manufacture if the material was used exclusively to produce much-needed postwar housing (rather than 500 Standard Oil gas stations, as had originally been suggested). By one account, nearly 2500 Lustrons were erected in 35 states east of the Rocky Mountains between 1948 and 1950. Buyers could choose from three basic models and from eight standard pastel exterior colors.

Lustron houses constructed in the Louisville area were sold by local dealer E. D. Cross and Co. to first-time homebuyers as starter homes. All but one were the two-bedroom Westchester model (the other models offered were the Newport and Meadowbrook). Company records have been located that indicate that the Cross dealership had assembled fifteen Lustrons by February, 1950 in the Louisville area. Fourteen sites of Lustrons have been located to date. The conditions of the homes currently on those sites range from Lustrons with architectural integrity to sites where the original home was destroyed or enveloped by new construction. The complete house was shipped in one "package" on a specially designed trailer from the main plant, a former Curtiss-Wright aircraft factory near Columbus, Ohio, to the local builder-dealer for speedy erection on the site. It took approximately ten days and cost from $6,500 to $10,500 for skilled assembly crews to erect each house. The Lustron Corp. boasted that the prefabricated building marvels, which had a steel roof and framing system and radiant heat panels situated in the ceilings, were "fireproof, ratproof...[and would never] fade, crack or peel, [and] never need painting, refinishing or reproofing" because the interior and exterior were made with interlocking, porcelain enamel-finished or steel panels similar to porcelain panels found on kitchen stoves and refrigerators. All surfaces could be wiped clean with a damp cloth, and pictures could be hung with magnets. Built-in cabinetry and a novel combination dishwasher-clothes washer that converted from one use to another "in a jiffy" were standard. The only parts of a Lustron home that were not steel were the aluminum window frames, asphalt floor

Photo by Louisville Metro Planning and Design

The Lustron homes still standing in the Louisville area in 2004 are located on Burwell Avenue (40210); Cambridge Drive (40214); Clarendon Avenue (40205); Dover Road (40206); Eleanor Avenue (40205); Fifth Avenue, LaGrange, KY (40010)*; Gladstone (40205); Greenwood Avenue (40211)**; North Hubbards Lane (40207); Old Forest Road, Pewee Valley, KY (40056)*; Southside Drive (40214); Westport Drive (40207); and Winston Avenue (40205).

* Lacks original architectural integrity
** may no longer be standing or may be enveloped by new building

University of Louisville Photographic Archives

tiles, and concrete foundations. The local Lustron dealership's first open house attracted an estimated ninety-six thousand visitors who watched salesmen shoot small metal cannonballs at a sample Lustron panel in an attempt to put to rest any questions about the material's durability. Sadly, the Lustron Corp. failed in 1950 because of multiple obstacles including political, financial, and production difficulties with local building codes, trade unions, and conventional builders.

Merriwether House is a familiar sight to drivers as they cross the old Harrod's Creek bridge on River Road.

MERRIWETHER HOUSE

Location/Address:	6421 River Road
Dates:	Circa 1898; addition 1950-74
Style:	Colonial Revival with an Eastland porch addition
Architect/Builder:	Harry Hall Merriwether, owner
Historic Status:	National Register of Historic Places

This simple two-story, wood frame house sits perched on a high, man-made terrace surrounded by mature trees on a plot of land close to the mouth of Harrods Creek. An elaborate Eastlake porch wraps around a basic Colonial Revival style house. It is a significant remnant of the early settlement of African Americans in Harrods Creek during the latter part of the 19th century. Owner Harry Hall Merriwether likely built it soon after 1898 when the records indicate he acquired the one-and-one-half acre site from his freed black grandfather, Harry Merriwether, for forty dollars. Although land holdings were small, the family engaged in raising crops and hogs, and tending a garden. In the early 20th century, as interest in recreational boating more fully developed along Harrods Creek, the Merriwether family constructed a dock and cottages to serve the boating public.

OLD LOUISVILLE DISTRICT

Location/Address:	South of Louisville Central Business District. Roughly bounded by portions of West Breckinridge Street, Interstate 65 North, portions of Hill Street and Cardinal Boulevard, and portions of Fifth Street and Seventh Street
Dates:	1880s-1910s
Style:	Late Victorian Eclectic including Chateauesque, Queen Anne, Princess Anne, Richardsonian Romanesque, Beaux-Arts, Italianate, Tudor, Classical Revival and Craftsman Bungalows
Architect/Builder:	Multiple
Historic Status:	Metro Landmark District, National Register of Historic Places

By 1868, the City of Louisville had extended its southern boundary to the area now occupied by the University of Louisville. But it was the Southern Exposition of 1883-1887, the largest manufacturing, farming and cultural exhibit ever held in the South, that served as the catalyst that spurred the development of Old Louisville. Although the Exposition buildings were demolished in 1888, infrastructure such as road improvements, electricity, and streetcar lines remained, making this outlying area accessible to land development. St. James and Belgravia Courts were built directly on the site of the dismantled Exposition center. St. James Court, dominated by a wide common lawn area in the center, was soon flanked by opulent houses displaying late Victorian excess. By 1892, Belgravia Court was developed as a pedestrian-only walking court. Although the houses along Belgravia were more closely spaced, they were no less grand. By 1899, more lots were sold and the area felt a major growth spurt. Soon there were many two- and three-story brick homes constructed not only on St. James and Belgravia Courts but on First through Sixth Streets as well. Homes would continue to be built well into the early 1900s.

Late Victorian eclectic styles found in the neighborhood include Chateauesque, Queen Anne, Princess Anne, Richardsonian Romanesque, Beaux-Arts, Italianate, Tudor, Classical Revival and Craftsman Bungalows. By the beginning of World War I, however, Old Louisville fell out of favor as outlying

areas on streetcar lines and later the automobile made those areas more accessible. New efficiencies and technological advances in electricity, plumbing, and heating made these homes appear obsolete by contrast. Soon these once grand residences were either being demolished or were being subdivided into smaller apartments or into offices. In 1961, Restoration Inc. was established to stem the tide of urban disinvestment. The group bought and renovated ten houses in the area. The plan worked, as interest in the area was renewed. Now Old Louisville is one of the most sought-after inner city addresses in Louisville. Old Louisville is among the largest National Register Districts in the United States and has one of the nation's most intact collections of Victorian architecture.

St. James Court and the entire surrounding area come to life every year on the first weekend of October for the St. James Court Art Show. It has become one of the largest open-air art shows in the country. Over a quarter million people attend the three-day event. Proceeds are used for the restoration, beautification and promotion of this beautiful neighborhood.

OLMSTED PARKS

Location/Address:	South, east and west quadrants of Louisville Metro
Dates:	1891-1935
Style:	Pastoral and Reform Era
Architects/Builders:	Frederick Law Olmsted, and successor firms
Historic Status:	National Register of Historic Places

Famed landscape architect Frederick Law Olmsted, who had achieved great reknown as the designer of Central Park in New York City, the Biltmore Estate and the U.S. Capitol Grounds, was invited by city leaders to author Louisville's park system in 1891. Olmsted's plan used a system of connecting parkways to link three major parks in distinct regions of the city: Iroquois, Shawnee and Cherokee. In conceiving each park design, Olmsted assessed the naturally-occurring character and contour of the land and strove to enhance it. At Iroquois Park in the south, Olmsted emphasized the deeply-forested hilly knob and sweeping vistas. At the western Shawnee Park, he worked with the river terraces to create promenades, gardens and parade grounds. At Cherokee Park to the east he took advantage of the rolling hills and stream valley for a purely scenic design. In all, Olmsted, his sons, and successor firms designed a total of eighteen parks and six parkways. They also worked on over 150 projects in the Louisville area that included landscape designs for subdivisions, private estates, institutions, clubs and businesses. Work of Olmsted and his successor firm is visible throughout the city.

Care for Louisville's Olmsted Parks is under the purview of the Louisville Metro Parks Department. Since 1989, the agency has partnered with Louisville Olmsted Parks Conservancy, a private, non-profit organization, to master plan and fund the rehabilitation of the Olmsted system.

Many generations of children have played at Big Rock in Cherokee Park.

Oxmoor

Location/Address:	7500 Shelbyville Road
Dates:	1787, 1829, 1915
Style:	Federal and Georgian Revival
Architects/Builders:	Alexander Scott Bullitt; William Christian Bullitt; William Marshall Bullitt; F. Burrall Hoffman, Jr., architect
Historic Status:	Metro Landmark, National Register of Historic Places

Oxmoor was the name given to the locality on Beargrass Creek in eastern Jefferson County that the Bullitt family purchased in 1787 and developed into a 1000-acre estate, where the principal crop was hemp. After living in a log house, Alexander Scott Bullitt built a modest frame house about 1791. His son, William Christian Bullitt, added a one-story, brick addition to the front in 1829. In 1914, his great-grandson, William Marshall Bullitt, retained New York architect F. Burrall Hoffman, Jr., to enlarge the house substantially by adding wings and making the main section two stories. The library wing was completed in 1927 to house Bullitt's extensive collection of history and mathematics books. Outbuildings include the slave kitchen, hemp house, icehouse, kitchen, and smokehouse, all in brick, as well as a stone springhouse and slave quarters. The family graveyard is nearby on land later added to Oxmoor that includes a two-story log house erected in 1785 by Mrs. Alexander Scott Bullitt's parents, William Christian and Anne Henry Christian, sister of Patrick Henry, as part of a cluster of pioneer structures known as A'Sturgus Station. Additional twentieth-century outbuildings dot the farm, which is still productive. The tree-lined approach to the residence and flower garden in the rear were conceived in 1911 by landscape architect Marian Cruger Coffin. In 1991, the Thomas Walker Bullitts donated in perpetuity a 79.3-acre preservation and conservation easement to the Commonwealth of Kentucky, through the Kentucky Heritage Council, that includes the homestead, which will be utilized in the future for research and educational purposes. The Filson Historical Society will assume ownership.

PARKLAND BUSINESS DISTRICT

Location/Address:	28th Street, centered roughly between Virginia Avenue and Dumesnil Street forms the spine of the business district. Portions of Catalpa and Olive Streets are also included.
Dates:	1890s-1920s
Style:	Early Twentieth Century Commercial
Architect/Builder:	Multiple
Historic Status:	Metro Landmark District, National Register of Historic Places

Parkland was laid out in 1871 and was incorporated as a town in 1879. In its early years the Parkland area was rural in character with three primary property owners and few structures. By 1884, however, the streets had been delineated and many residences had been constructed. Between 1884 and 1890, Parkland was considered a fashionable and prestigious streetcar suburb of Louisville. Housing stock reflected the fashions of the day and included examples of brick and frame structures built in the Italianate, Queen Anne and Craftsman Bungalow styles. The scale of residences varied from small shotgun houses to elaborate multi-story residences. Early success of development of Parkland can be attributed to town ordinances that prohibited drinking and rowdy behavior. Parkland also had five churches and a Masonic temple to fulfill area residence's social and spiritual needs.

In 1890, however, a tornado tore through the area destroying or damaging many homes. Rebuilding commenced almost immediately and the town was annexed by the City of Louisville in 1894. To serve the thriving community, a small commercial district developed. The Masonic Hall (first built in 1889 and replaced in 1923) at the south end of 28th Street served as the district's focal point to the south while the Parkland Branch Library, built with Carnegie funds, (1908) anchored the business district to the north. The Washburn Building, constructed by African American architect and contractor Samuel Plato, was built in 1930 to serve the area's need for retail and office space. In recent years there has been a mix of new construction amid the historic buildings in the area.

This view of Parkland (28th and Dumesnil) is from the 1920s. While the larger Parkland neighborhood is listed in the National Register of Historic Places, only the small commercial district is a designated Historic Preservation District.

The Peterson-Dumesnil House is located on Peterson Avenue, one of Louisville's last brick streets, originally built to maximize traction for early automobiles.

PETERSON-DUMESNIL HOUSE

Location/Address:	301 Peterson Avenue
Dates:	1869-70
Style:	Italianate
Architect/Builder:	Henry Whitestone, attributed
Historic Status:	Metro Landmark, National Register of Historic Places

The Peterson-Dumesnil House is located in Louisville's Crescent Hill Neighborhood and was built for Joseph Peterson, a tobacco wholesaler, around 1869-70. The architecture of the house is characterized by its tall, narrow windows that present a strong vertical emphasis, prominent door and window hoods topped with segmental arches, projecting cornice replete with brackets, consoles and dentils, and the octagonal cupola and finial that top the building. It is a fine example of the Italian Villa style popularized by the publications of A.J Downing's *The Architecture of Country Houses* and Calvert Vaux's *Villas and Cottages*. Each book extolled the virtues of how picturesque and suitable the Italianate Villa style was for a country home of the mid-19th century. Peterson, who lived in the house until his death, passed it down to his granddaughters, one of whom married Harry Dumesnil. Thus, the name Dumesnil has been integrated into the place name as it was passed down from one Dumesnil family member to another. There is speculation, but no hard evidence, that noted Louisville architect Henry Whitestone may have designed this country residence. The house passed from the Dumesnil family in 1948 to the Louisville Board of Education. In 1977, the school board leased it to the Crescent Hill Neighborhood Association. When the Louisville-Jefferson County Board of Education declared the property surplus in 1982, a foundation was established to raise the necessary funds to purchase the neighborhood landmark. After two years, title was transferred to the Crescent Hill Community Council and it is now managed by the Peterson-Dumesnil House Foundation, Inc. for community events and rentals.

PORTLAND NEIGHBORHOOD

Location/Address:	Bound by the Ohio River, Tenth Street, Market Street, and Interstate 264
Dates:	Laid out in 1811 based on plans by surveyor William Lytle; annexed by the City of Louisville in 1852
Style:	Federal, Greek Revival, Vernacular, Victorian Eclectic (including Queen Anne, Princess Anne, Steamboat Gothic, Tudor Revival,
Architect/Builder:	Multiple
Historic Status:	National Register of Historic Places

French and Irish immigrants founded the Portland neighborhood located in Louisville's far northwestern reaches, in 1814. Portland, along with nearby Shippingport, served as a port of entry and departure for travelers and cargo that plied the Ohio River. It was laid out as a riverport based on plans drawn by surveyor William Lytle in 1811. By 1819, Portland was a major port town that rivaled Louisville in size and commerce. The wharfs thrived because of trading generated by steamboat landings. As commerce increased, more and more commercial establishments opened up. Warehousing provided cargo storage and foundries and shipyards dotted the river's edge. Hotels, saloons, gambling houses, and outfitters all did a brisk business. Those wishing an alternative to river travel could use the Portland-Louisville turnpike, which served as an early overland route to and from the area. Construction of a canal, designed to bypass Portland, was completed by 1830. During this time, commerce in the area continued to grow and, in 1834, Portland was officially established. By 1852, Louisville had surpassed Portland in size and as a result annexed the town. River commerce and the workers related to it populated the town and built homes with strong architectural references to the Ohio River. While wealthy steamboat captains, ship owners and entrepreneurs built grand brick and frame residences, stevedores and roustabouts built smaller shotgun houses. Many sported the decorative bargeboard and Eastlake details common to steamboat architecture. By 1871, however, Portland's commercial enterprise faded, as commerce lessened after the Portland Canal was deepened and widened to accommodate larger vessels. Floods have plagued Portland through the years with those of 1937 and

By the early 1800s, Portland was a bustling river town that attracted both French and Irish immigrants.

1945 proving the most damaging. The resultant construction of a floodwall along Rudd Avenue to stem the tide of the river flow has all but cut the community of Portland off from its river roots. Construction of Interstate 64 has provided another barrier between the former port town and the river as well. Despite these changes, remnants of Portland's river past suggest a comprehensive image of this area in the 19th century. Area landmarks include the 1841 Catholic church, Notre Dame du Port (Church of Our Lady) at 3511 Rudd Avenue, the 1852 United States Marine Hospital at 2214 Northwestern Parkway, the circa 1811-1827 Earick House at 719 North 34th Street, the circa 1830 Portland Cemetery at 3305 Northwestern Parkway, the circa 1860 Captain James Irvin House at 2901 Northwestern Parkway, and the 1913 Carnegie-endowed Portland Branch Library at 3305 Northwestern Parkway.

The thoughtful, current restoration of Ridgeway was begun by owners Benjamin M. and Carole Birkhead after their purchase of the property in 1977.

RIDGEWAY

Location/Address:	4095 Ridgeway Avenue
Dates:	Constructed circa 1816-1818; modernized by Frederick Lindley Morgan, 1922; restoration begun by owners, Benjamin M. and Carole Birkhead after their purchase in 1977
Style:	Federal
Architect/Builder:	Unknown
Historic Status:	Metro Landmark, National Register of Historic Places

Ridgeway has been described by many as the finest federal-style residence in the Commonwealth of Kentucky. Ridgeway is a brick house laid in a Flemish bond pattern. The house was reportedly built by slaves assisted by journeymen carpenters using bricks made from clay dug and fired on site. Ridgeway is bilaterally symmetrical in plan and features an elongated footprint that measures 40 yards by 40 feet. It is composed of a central block flanked by subordinate wings that are connected into a unified mass by recessed hyphens. All are topped by a hipped roof arrangement. The entrance features a double door flanked by sidelights and topped by an elliptical fanlight. A pediment adorned with a delicate lunette window tops a columned Doric portico. The interior features a transverse hallway, several elliptical doorways, and delicately hand-carved mantels and woodwork. In the basement is a cock-fighting pit. Surveyor Colonel Henry Massie and his wife, Helen Scott Bullitt (daughter of Kentucky's first Lieutenant Governor, Alexander Scott Bullitt) constructed the house between 1816 and 1818. After Henry's death in 1830 Helen, (who remained childless) went on to marry two more times. In 1834 she married J. L. Martin (reportedly the richest man in Kentucky) and in 1857 she married Marshall Key (brother to Francis Scott Key). In both cases, a prenuptial agreement disavowed inheritance rights to their spouse's property. Upon her death in 1872, Ridgeway and its 434 acres of land were parceled off and passed on to her heirs. Ridgeway was eventually bought by the Kaelin family who established Ridgeway Farms, a dairy concern. In 1922 the house was purchased by Aubrey and Maud Woodson Cossar who hired noted local architect Frederick Lindley Morgan to install modern conveniences such as electricity, plumbing and mechanical systems.

RIVERSIDE, THE FARNSLEY-MOREMEN LANDING

Location/Address:	10908 Lower River Road at Moorman Road
Date:	Circa 1837
Style:	Greek Revival
Architect/Builder:	Gabriel Farnsley, owner
Historic Status:	Metro Landmark, National Register of Historic Places

Riverside, The Farnsley-Moremen Landing is an historic house and farm located in southwest Jefferson County. This brick I-house, which faces the Ohio River and features a two-story Greek Revival style porch, is the focal point of a parcel of land that currently totals more than 300 acres. Gabriel Farnsley built the house on the Ohio River 13 miles south of Louisville in about 1837. Not only did Farnsley, with the help of slave labor, raise livestock and crops that he traded with passengers on passing riverboats, he also operated a ferry used to transport goods and people from southwest Jefferson County across the Ohio to southern Indiana.

Farnsley died in 1849 with no will and no children. After several years of legal wrangling, in 1862 Alanson and Rachel Moremen purchased the house. The Moremens eventually increased the farm holdings to over 1500 acres. In 1879 they renamed their farm "Riverside" to reflect its geographic placement. Records indicate the house stayed under Moremen family ownership for 126 years. The Moremens continued to operate the ferryboat and eventually began selling lye soap and other household goods to riverboat men. Soon, this enterprise became known as Soap Landing. To aid their efforts, they also used slave labor and had one of the largest slave holdings in the area.

It was purchased by Jefferson County Fiscal Court in 1988 and was opened to the public in 1993. In 1999 a modern riverboat landing was constructed to allow for riverboat excursions. Extensive archeological investigations to ascertain the locations of agricultural outbuildings are ongoing. The farm complex is being restored to reflect the agricultural and river heritage of southwest Jefferson County.

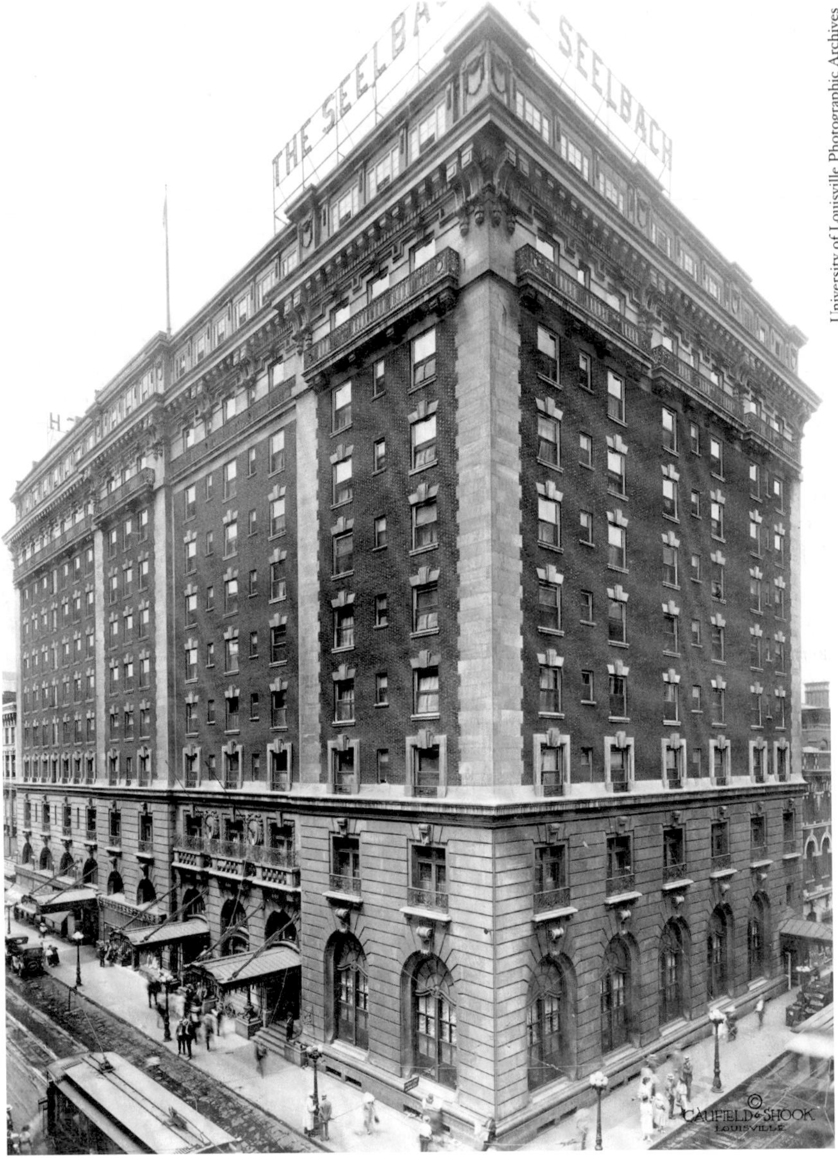

University of Louisville Photographic Archives

THE SEELBACH HOTEL

Location/Address:	500 South Fourth Street
Date:	1905
Style:	Beaux-Arts
Architects/Builders:	William J. Dodd and Frank M. Andrews
Historic Status:	National Register of Historic Places

Louisville's grand Seelbach Hotel, located at the busy intersection of Fourth and Muhammad Ali Boulevard (formerly Walnut Street), was completed in 1905. It was built as the brainchild of German immigrant brothers Louis and Otto Seelbach, who wanted to replace an earlier Seelbach Hotel situated at Sixth and Main Streets. Architects William J. Dodd of Louisville and Frank M. Andrews of Dayton, Ohio teamed up to conceive the opulent ten-story, Beaux-Arts style design. The new Seelbach Hotel was lavishly furnished. Murals depicting pioneers by artist Arthur Thomas, who specialized in Native American art, graced the lobby walls. Richly-appointed restaurant and bar areas were outfitted with Oriental rugs and hardwood from the West Indies. The Seelbach also boasted the city's first roof garden. The Rathskeller, a popular underground entertainment and banquet space, was appointed with walls veneered entirely with tiles by the famous Rookwood pottery company of Cincinnati. A rarity, it is the world's only extant Rookwood room. The tenth floor ballroom is of the Georgian style. A host of famous people have passed through its doors, including F. Scott Fitzgerald, who reported to duty at nearby Camp Zachary Taylor on March 15, 1918 to be trained as a World War I soldier. The author makes a thinly-veiled reference to the Seelbach, calling it the "Muhlbach" Hotel in his 1925 book *The Great Gatsby*. In it, Fitzgerald details how Tom Buchanan stayed at the hotel when he came to Louisville in 1919 to marry Daisy Fay. Early years of popularity and financial success for the Seelbach were followed by financial troubles, and by 1975 the Seelbach closed its doors. After several failed attempts were made to reinvigorate the Seelbach, it was purchased in 1978 by builder/developer Gil Whittenberg and actor and Louisville native Roger Davis. They restored the building to its former glory, and after four years of meticulous renovation the structure re-opened in 1982.

The exterior of the shotgun house often features such amenities as partial or full-width front porches, elaborate window and door surrounds, gingerbread trim, and stained or leaded glass windows. Shotgun houses are one of Louisville's most abundant house types and are tangible reminders of solidly built, attractive, late-19th and early-20th century worker housing. They remain one of our most viable and adaptable buildings.

SHOTGUN HOUSES

Location/Address:	Working class neighborhoods throughout Louisville
Dates:	Predominantly 1860s-1910s
Style:	Vernacular, Italianate, Princess Anne, and Classical Revival are among the most common
Architects/Builders:	Built by contractors and builders; rarely architect-designed
Historic Status:	Many are listed in the National Register of Historic Places as elements of neighborhood districts and are located in Local Preservation Districts

The shotgun house, a common residential building type found in many of Louisville's historic working class neighborhoods, can best be described as a modest, rectangular structure that is typically one story high, one room wide, and three to four rooms deep. By some estimates shotgun houses comprise ten percent of Louisville's building stock. The majority of local examples were built between the end of the Civil War, when the city was experiencing a period of post-War industrial expansion, and 1910. Particularly strong concentrations can be found in the Portland, Phoenix Hill, Smoketown, Butchertown, Germantown, Schnitzelberg, Russell, California, and lower Highlands neighborhoods.

Oral tradition attributes its name to the distinct floor plan: the linear alignment of all exterior and interior doors allows a person to stand at the front door of the house, shoot a shotgun, and have its pellets pass through each of the building's rooms and out the back door without ricocheting off any interior wall. Most of Louisville's shotgun houses are constructed of wood frame or brick (although some stone examples exist) and are topped by a hipped or front-facing gabled roof. Typically the front room serves as the living room with the bedroom in the middle and the kitchen to the rear. Often, the side windows face the windowless side of the house next door, adding an unusual element of privacy. To this basic building form a variety of Victorian architectural revival styles are applied: Italianate, Princess Anne, and Classical Revival are among the most common.

Springfield, once home to President Zachary Taylor, is one of very few presidential residences still in private hands. Once a large farm tract, Springfield has now been enveloped by suburban neighborhoods in the east end of Louisville.

SPRINGFIELD
THE ZACHARY TAYLOR HOME

Location/Address:	5608 Apache Road
Dates:	Circa 1785, with additions circa 1810 or 1820, and post-tornado restoration in 1974
Style:	Georgian
Architect/Builder:	Colonel Richard Taylor, owner
Historic Status:	National Historic Landmark, National Register of Historic Places

Springfield, childhood home to Zachary Taylor, twelfth president of the United States, is one of the oldest houses in Louisville Metro and is an excellent local example of Georgian architecture. It sits on what was originally a 400-acre land tract that was later increased to 700 acres, and more recently reduced to approximately one-half acre. This two-story house was built in two building campaigns: the first section was built around 1785 in the Georgian style while a two-story brick wing was added around 1810 or 1820. Many of the home's original interior details remain intact. Taylor lived at Springfield until 1808 when he left Louisville to join the military. He returned often and, upon his death, was buried in a family cemetery that is now part of the adjacent Zachary Taylor National Cemetery. Springfield is one of the country's few presidential homes that have remained a private residence. In 1974, it was heavily damaged during a devastating tornado but was sensitively restored soon thereafter. National Historic Landmark status was bestowed on the property based on its association with President Taylor.

THE STARKS BUILDING

Location/Address:	455 South Fourth
Dates:	1913, 1926
Style:	Chicago School, Beaux-Arts influences
Architect/Builder:	D.H. Burnham and Company; with an addition by Graham, Anderson, Probst and White
Historic Status:	National Register of Historic Places

The Starks Building has been a familiar landmark to Louisvillians since its construction at the corner of Fourth Street and Muhammed Ali Boulevard (formerly Walnut Street) in 1913. The Starks Building stands as a monument to the Chicago School of architecture. Technological advances of the turn of the century are reflected in the structure's emphasis on verticality while the tradition associated with Burnham's work at Chicago's Colombian Exposition of 1893 is displayed by repeated use of classical motifs. It was designed by D. H. Burnham and Company of Chicago with an addition by Burnham successor firm, Graham, Anderson, Probst and White. John Price Starks commissioned Burnham to design a mixed-use office in part due to the recognition the architect had received as one of the leading promoters and planners/architects of the 1893 World's Colombian Exposition held in Chicago. It was under architect William LaBaron Jenny, widely recognized as father of the modern skyscraper, that Burnham learned the architectural basics. He later partnered with John Wellborn Root, and upon Root's death, formed D. H. Burnham and Company.

Burnham's Starks Building reflects the Chicago School tradition popularized by Louis Sullivan and the neo-Classicism inspired by the Colombian Exposition. "Form follows function," the mantra of Louis Sullivan, is manifested in the visual strength of the widened piers at the building's corners and the implied pilasters delineating each bay which emphasizes verticality. With a bow to the Beaux-Arts tradition, the Starks Building's form follows the order of a classical column with base topped by shaft topped by capital. Its conservatism reflects the classics while still expressing progressive ideals of Sullivan's Chicago School. The 1926 addition enclosed one end of the U-shaped building to form a four-sided structure. A dramatic light court allows for light infiltration on floors two through fifteen.

Early promotional literature touted the importance of the Starks Building for its strategic location "at the intersection of two principal transportation arteries, in the heart of the retail district."

The highly innovative and experimental Triaero, built over 60 years ago, is intact and located in the Fern Creek area of Louisville. Architect Jack Neuschwander and his wife, Mary, have been restoring Triaero since their purchase of the property in 1992.

TRIAERO

Location/Address:	8310 Johnson School Road
Dates:	1942, partially rebuilt/modified in 1959, currently under restoration.
Style:	Modern/Usonian
Architect/Builder:	Bruce Goff

In 1941, at age 37, Bruce Goff, a young architect from Chicago, was hired by Fern Creek, Kentucky resident Irma Bartman to design a vacation retreat. Inspired by spectacular views 120 degrees apart, the architect chose a triangular plan with an abundance of glass, a bold statement for the time. He called his design "Triaero" because of the triangular floor plan and winged appearance. This so called "airplane" house was to be one of Goff's crowning achievements. It remains amazingly modern-looking, even by today's standards.

The building's cantilevered construction allows the building to hang from its central structural and utility core and also allows for inordinate amounts of glass. Within its walls there is a scant 970 feet of living space.

Triaero has many unique features. Triangles are used as a design theme throughout the house. Copper sheeting secured with redwood battens gives the house a horizontal, linear quality. Pipe props at the buildings' corners stabilize Triaero for wind gusts and tornado-strength winds. Triangular reflecting pools viewed through the floor-to-ceiling plate glass windows bring the outside in. Aside from the triangular utility core (which houses the tiny galley kitchen, a bath, and the mechanical systems) there are absolutely no interior walls. This allows for flexible use of space. All of the house's furniture was custom made for the architect.

Although it was heavily damaged by fire in the 1950s, the basic form is still intact. The restored firepit is sunk a foot below floor level. Goff actually designed a combination patio/garage so that multiple users could be served depending on the owner's needs. One could actually drive a car into the house! Goff and Bartman brainstormed and decided that Triaero would be an inspiration to them. Together, they planned to erect an entire subdivision of houses in geometric shapes, but future subdivision plans were changed by World War II.

UNION STATION

Location/Address:	1000 West Broadway
Dates:	1889-91
Style:	Richardsonian Romanesque
Architect/Builder:	F.W. Mowbray
Historic Status:	Metro Landmark, National Register of Historic Places

Union Station was dedicated in 1891 as the city's largest passenger train terminal. Designed in the Richardsonian Romanesque style, it is the largest commercial example of that style in the city. Prominent eastern architect F. W. Mowbray was brought to Louisville with the express purpose of providing design expertise to the railroad terminal project. The façade of Union Station is dominated by a central, stained glass, rose window. Inside, a massive barrel-vaulted terminal space greets the visitor. Originally the central concourse was equipped with dining rooms and ticket counters. Wrought iron was used to trim the second floor balcony space where the terminal offices were located. The entire complex, including tracks, platforms, train shed, baggage room and passenger service support facilities, was located within a 40-acre campus.

Union Station originally served as a train station, first for the Louisville and Nashville Railroad, and later for Amtrak. Nearly every immigrant to Louisville, and countless servicemen and women, including General Pershing and three United States Presidents (Franklin D. Roosevelt, Harry S. Truman and Dwight D. Eisenhower), entered the city through Union Station's doors. Until the mid-1960s, Union Station was an especially popular point of arrival and departure for numerous Kentucky Derby guests who arrived on Pullman sleepers or private rail cars to begin their Derby festivities. In 1976, rail service to Union Station ceased.

The Louisville and Nashville Railroad sold the passenger rail complex to the Transit Authority of River City (TARC), Louisville's bus service company. The restoration, which started in April 1979 and was completed in one year, cost about $2 million.

Plans are currently underway to return the U.S. Marine Hospital to a public use so that it might become the focal point for revitalization of the surrounding Portland neighborhood. From the cupola visitors could once again experience the restorative view that convalescing watermen saw when they gazed out over the Portland Canal toward the Ohio River.

UNITED STATES MARINE HOSPITAL

Location/Address:	2214 Northwestern Parkway
Dates:	1845-52
Style:	Greek Revival, hospital; Italianate, stable; Mission style, laundry building
Architects/Builders:	Robert Mills, Major Stephen Harriman Long, Corps of Engineers architects and engineers
Historic Status:	National Historic Landmark, Metro Landmark, National Register of Historic Places

The United States Marine Hospital is a reminder of Portland's and Louisville's river history at the Falls of the Ohio. It is a survivor from the days of steamboats, the engineering of the Portland Canal, and the construction of the McAlpine Locks.

The Marine Hospital was constructed between 1845 and 1852 and is almost entirely intact. It was a prototype design for the seven U.S. Marine Hospitals funded by Congress to address health needs of seamen on the Western Waterways. When the hospital was built, the Ohio River was a major transportation artery and America's "interstate highway system." It was designed by Robert Mills, the first professionally-trained architect born in America, and it is the only surviving example of inland marine hospitals in the country. Construction of the building was supervised by Major Stephen Harriman Long, one of the great early explorers of the Rocky Mountains and a leading expert in railroad designs. While working on the U.S. Marine Hospital, Long was also involved in planning improvements on the nearby Portland Canal. Later Corps of Engineers architects and engineers modified the design during construction. Mills was a highly-regarded federal architect who designed the Washington Monument, the U.S. Treasury Building and the Old Post Office in Washington D.C. He learned his trade under the tutelage of Thomas Jefferson and Benjamin Henry Latrobe. The Louisville-Jefferson County Metro Health Department assumed ownership of the building in 1976. It was designated a National Historic Landmark in 1997 on the basis of maritime history and public health history. The National Trust for Historic Preservation named the U.S. Marine Hospital to its 2003 list of America's Eleven Most Endangered Historic Places. It is also designated a "Save America's Treasures" building by the National Park Service.

LOUISVILLE WATER COMPANY PUMPING STATION/THE WATER TOWER

Photo by Louisville Metro Planning and Design

Location/Address:	3005 Upper River Road
Dates:	1858-60
Style:	Greek Revival
Architect/Builder:	Theodore Scowden
Historic Status:	National Historic Landmark, National Register of Historic Places

The Louisville Water Company's pumping station and its 169-foot tall water tower, both designed by chief engineer Theodore Scowden, were constructed and pumping water for the citizens of Louisville by 1860. Both are architectural and engineering landmarks.

The waterworks is a Greek Revival, two-story brick building. Its most striking feature is the front portico adorned with colossal Corinthian columns topped by a pediment. In front of the waterworks building is a standpipe tower designed in the form of a giant Greek column. The base of the standpipe is ringed with a Corinthian colonnade, topped by a balustrade, and accentuated by statues. Nine of the statues are classical in design while the tenth is an American Indian standing beside his dog.

The substantial amount of flat ground surrounding the Water Tower has served as athletic fields, fair and festival grounds, an outdoor concert venue, and public gathering space, and is an important civic amenity. The Louisville Visual Art Association's gallery space is located in the main building, and its annual gathering to watch the Great Steamboat Race during the Kentucky Derby Festival is one of Louisville's largest outdoor parties.

Louisville Water Works
Crescent Hill Reservoir

Location/Address:	Reservoir Avenue, between Frankfort Avenue and Brownsboro Road
Date:	1879
Style:	Gothic Revival
Architect/Builder:	Charles Hermany
Historic Status:	National Register of Historic Places

The original water reservoir located on a high bluff above the Water Company Pumping Station on River Road was replaced by 1879, due to increased city demand for water. The new reservoir, designed by Theodore Scowden's successor, Charles Hermany, was built in Crescent Hill between Brownsboro Road and Frankfort Avenue. The new reservoir had a capacity of 100 million gallons—14 times larger than the original reservoir. Pipelines connecting the Pumping Station and the reservoir, still operating today, were laid under Pipe Line Avenue, since renamed Zorn Avenue.

The reservoir buildings were designed in the Gothic Revival style and are ornamented with beautiful stone tracery and iron cresting. Stone pitchers adorn the roofline of the Reservoir's pump house building. Two settling basins surrounded by a decorative iron railing flank it.

Like the Pumping Station to its north, the reservoir grounds are used as public recreation space, with generations of Louisvillians having used the cement pathways around the reservoir as a walking/jogging track.

West Main Street District

Location/Address:	Portions of West Main Street from the 300 Block to just east of Ninth Street
Dates:	1860s-1900 (major growth period between 1880-1900)
Style:	Federal, Italianate, Richardsonian Romanesque, Victorian Eclectic
Architect/Builder:	Multiple
Historic Status:	Metro Landmark District, National Register of Historic Places

Main Street in Louisville was the city's original east-west street and an important link between the Louisville Wharf that served the upper Ohio River from Pittsburgh and the Portland/Shippingport wharfs serving river traffic down to New Orleans. Main Street grew in importance and commercial activity when steamboat traffic (starting in 1811 with Nicholas Roosevelt's first downriver cruise) began moving massive amounts of produce, manufactured foods, and passengers down the Ohio River. In 1815, Captain Henry Shreve's initial upriver voyage from New Orleans encouraged import of southern products to the American Midwest. Louisville stood at the crossroads of commerce, transportation, and industry.

But with rise of rail transport later in the 19th century, the traditional river commerce in Louisville began a downward spiral. By the early 20th century Main Street was lifeless. It was not until the 1970s with the movement to rediscover the Ohio River as the city's historic focal point that this trend began to reverse. Early linchpins to the area's revitalization included the Galt House Hotel complex, Actors Theater of Louisville, the Humana Tower, the Kentucky Center for the Arts, and the Louisville Science Center. More recently, the Hillerich and Bradsby baseball bat factory, the Frazier Historical Arms Museum, and the new Brown-Forman Headquarters Building have located on West Main.

Architecturally, West Main Street is known primarily for its high concentration of cast iron storefronts. They were constructed primarily in the late 19th century when Louisville boasted eleven iron foundries and was the largest cast iron manufacturing center in the nation.

A stroll down Main Street, particularly in the 500 to 800 blocks, will reveal the Louisville Metro government's initiative to interpret this area as a

Cultural Arts District. Louisville has the second highest concentration of cast iron architecture in America, second only to SoHo in New York City. Note the cast iron tree guards installed as both a downtown beautification and interpretative measure. Each tree guard was designed to reflect the historic use of the building to which it connects.

The decorative cast iron coal hole covers embedded in the sidewalks cover the former coal chutes for businesses in the area. Sidewalk place mats also appear at the thresholds of many buildings in this area and were designed to reflect historic uses of these magnificent buildings.

WOLF PEN BRANCH MILL

Location/Address:	8117 Wolf Pen Branch Road
Date:	Circa 1870s
Style:	Industrial
Architect/Builder:	Herman Miller, owner
Historic Status:	Metro Landmark, National Register of Historic Places

Wolf Pen Branch Mill is a mid-1800s mill, noted as the oldest surviving industrial structure still standing in Jefferson County. It is located on Wolf Pen Branch, a tributary to Harrods Creek. The present stone structure replaced an earlier stone or log mill that was destroyed by a flood in the 1850s. Herman Miller supposedly financed construction of this mill by selling butterbeans to support the effort. The mill itself is constructed of rough-cut fieldstone laid in a random fashion that is set without mortar. Only the third and fourth stories of the four-story structure are visible from below the mill chase. A 26-foot overshot wooden water wheel is located directly below the stone section. Water from a millpond is directed through a channel. The force of the water propels the wheel which, in turn, rotates about five or six revolutions per minute. With each revolution, grinding stones then turn, grinding the corn into meal. In 1999 the mill's owner, Sallie Bingham, donated the 412 acres surrounding the mill as a conservation easement held by River Fields and the Kentucky Heritage Council.

Bibliography

Altrusa Society. *Cut, Cast and Carved*. Louisville: Altrusa Society, 1974.

Brown, Theodore M. *Introduction to Louisville Architecture*. Louisville: Louisville Free Public Library, 1960.

Brown, Theodore M., and Margaret M. Bridwell. *Old Louisville: The Architecture, The People, Architectural Conservation*. Louisville: University of Louisville, 1961.

Cullinane, John, and Margaret A. Thomas. *Walking Through Louisville*. Louisville: Data Courier, Inc., 1976.

Karem, Anne. *The Cherokee Area: A History*. Louisville: Mrs. David K. Karem, 1971.

Karem, Kenny. *Discover Louisville: An Illustrated Activity Guidebook for Exploring City and County Neighborhoods*. Louisville: Louisville Historical League, 1988.

Kleber, John E., ed. *The Encyclopedia of Louisville*. Louisville: The University Press of Kentucky, 2001.

Kramer, Carl. *Louisville Survey Central and South Report*. Louisville: City of Louisville, Community Development Cabinet, 1978.

Kramer, Carl. *Louisville Survey East Report*. Louisville: City of Louisville, Community Development Cabinet, 1979.

Langsam, Walter E., ed. *Preservation: Louisville Metropolitan Architectural and Historic Preservation Plan*. Louisville: Falls of the Ohio Metropolitan Council of Governments, May 1973.

Louisville-Jefferson County Metro Historic Landmarks and Preservation Districts Commission Collection.

Morgan, William. *Louisville: Architecture and the Urban Environment*. Dublin, NH: W.I. Bauhan, 1979.

Neary, Donna M., ed. *Historic Jefferson County*. Louisville: Jefferson County Fiscal Court, 2000.

Nomination Forms. Washington: National Register of Historic Places, US Department of the Interior, National Park Service, n.d.

Rogers, John C. *The Story of Louisville Neighborhoods*. Louisville: The Courier-Journal and Louisville Times, 1955.

The Shotgun House: Urban Housing Opportunities. Louisville: Preservation Alliance of Louisville and Jefferson County, Inc., 1980.

Thomas, Samuel W., and William Morgan. *Old Louisville: The Victorian Era*. Louisville: Data Courier, Inc. for the Courier-Journal and Louisville Times, 1975.

Thomas, Samuel W., ed. *Views of Louisville Since 1766*. Louisville: The Courier-Journal and Louisville Times, 1971.

Yater, George H. *Two Hundred Years at the Falls of the Ohio: A History of Louisville and Jefferson County*. Louisville: The Heritage Corporation, 1979.